T0248050

WARRIOR SELLING

WARRIOR SELLING

The **12 STEPS** to Achieving a
100 Percent Conversion Rate

Jason Forrest

Skyhorse Publishing

To anyone who joins me on the mission to ignite the pride, purpose, and respect for the profession of sales!

Contents

Acknowledgments

Thank you to the following FPG teammates who helped bring this book to print:

- Aley Salcedo
- Eric De La Rosa
- Kathy Kender
- Laurie McCullar
- Jacqui Faber
- Zaither Rueda

Thank you to my kids: Saunders, Mary Jane, and Elisabeth, for all of your love and support.

My greatest appreciation goes to Mary Marshall Forrest. You are so many people to me:

- As the senior editor, you have up-leveled every page of this book through your genius way of communicating my vision in a simple and easy way for everyone to learn.
- As the chief learning officer, you have field-tested with our clients every concept taught in this book to ensure that everything we teach only leads sales warriors to become their very best and give them an advantage in all circumstances.
- As my wife, you have unrivaled belief in me and my mission to ignite the pride, purpose, and respect for professional sales.
- As my girlfriend, with our weekly date nights, you ground me so I can understand, every week, what really matters.
- As my best friend, you speak your highest truth to me and push me to achieve my greatest purpose.

Introduction

Right now, you are reading this book for one of three reasons:

- You are new to sales and looking to adopt a step-by-step process that will help you dominate in your new career.
- You are a salesperson experiencing a slump, and you are looking for solutions.
- You are in the top 1 percent as a salesperson and are always seeking leading-edge sales techniques and resources to give you a competitive advantage.

Wherever you are in your sales career right now, this book will help. I can tell you with 100 percent confidence that if you experience inconsistency throughout the year, struggle to handle objections, lose customers to the competition, or even want a structured resource to keep you at the top of your game, then this book is for you. I wrote this book for one sole purpose: to show you a way to achieve the highest conversion rate—no matter the economic climate, circumstance, or situation.

A consistent process will be the key to your improved conversion rate. An inconsistent sales process leads to inconsistent results, which leads to uncertainty in your sales forecast. *Harvard Business Review* found that companies that defined a formal sales process experienced 18 percent more revenue growth than companies that didn't.[1] And guess what? Those companies *that executed* that research *performed at an even higher growth percentage.* This is nuts, right? Just having a formal sales process without the accountability of execution showed an 18 percent revenue growth. Can you imagine what would happen to your own sales if you both read this sales process and implemented it? Right now, do the math to figure out what an 18 percent raise this year would be for you. Use that as your motivation to implement the ideas you read in this book.

This book provides a bulletproof sales process for you. It was created from my own personal experiences in sales, distilling the best ideas from leading sales experts, and refined by studying hundreds of sales warriors across every industry you can imagine. I can promise you that everything in this book has been personally vetted by myself, my sales team, and the hundreds of clients and thousands of salespeople that FPG has worked with over the last fifteen years. There is a reason FPG is ranked a Top Sales Training Program in the World by Global Gurus, a research organization and the top website for the world's best thought leaders, teachers, trainers, and speakers globally.[2]

I've stripped down my award-winning ninety-day Warrior Selling Training program to the basics and provided it here in *Warrior Selling* for you to adopt as your new sales process. The process will meet your current circumstances and any situation in the years to come. Its twelve steps will teach you how to understand your customer's mission on a deeper level, to present solutions without fear or hesitation, and to remove ambiguity to resolve your sales. The process that you walk away with will continue to be relevant, so you can continue to sell through any season, situation, or circumstance.

Most sales training and books are based on somebody's opinion; the author is writing a book to teach the world to sell in the way that the author wants to buy. *Warrior Selling* is different. It is not my opinion. It was not created based on my preferences. Every step in this process is backed by research that shows the *majority* of people respond positively to this method of selling. The research comes from BSRP, the leading research company on the science of selling; from neurolinguistic programming (NLP); and the work of many different psychologists. Each of the twelve steps in *Warrior Selling* uses research from the Behavioral Sciences Research Press or from NLP metaprograms that prove a correlation to closing sales. I urge you to read this book with confidence that the steps have a proven correlation to closing more sales, when executed correctly. I want you to feel confident in the twelve steps knowing that every bit of this process is backed by science, showing the majority of people will respond positively to this approach.

More important, this process was not just created by scientists and theorists but also by studying practitioners. These practitioners are among the top 20 percent of sales professionals across more than forty industries that we serve. (We call them Sales Warriors.) We observed and interviewed them to clearly understand how they think, behave, and speak. Next, we field-tested the approach through our own use of the steps when selling FPG's sales recruiting and sales training services. Once we were comfortable that we had a winning process, we gave it to our clients. As of this writing, thousands of sales professionals across forty different industries have learned and executed the twelve steps to Warrior Selling, with record results. We did all of this to ensure that everything in this book makes up the most relevant—and most successful—sales process.

I'll say to you what I say to all my clients: I'm not in the business of making salespeople worse or poorer. If you need a little more convincing, here are several of the over forty industries (as of this publication) represented by those who have gone through our Warrior Selling program successfully and have provided testimonies affirming their success:

- residential construction
- fifty-five-plus homebuilding
- forward mortgages
- reverse mortgages
- gold and precious metals
- industrial machinery and equipment/heavy construction machinery
- commercial construction
- pension fund
- commercial concrete
- engineering services
- fitness and yoga
- architectural and interior design services
- concrete and masonry staining
- environmental goods and services
- luxury mattresses
- luxury automobiles
- health care
- commercial and residential furniture
- commercial and residential roofing
- commercial HVAC
- sporting and recreational equipment, retail
- commercial fleet tracking
- loss prevention
- learning technology
- senior living and assisted care

- cremation services
- management consulting
- recruiting and headhunting
- military recruiting
- plastic reusable containers, pallets, and bins
- plastics for recreational marine, agricultural, and military vehicles
- commercial distribution
- motor vehicle manufacturing
- marketing and advertising
- software as a service over the internet (SAAS)
- lawn design and construction
- commercial and residential real estate
- human resources
- banking and financial services
- wholesale residential lumber and building materials
- commercial and residential security
- translation and linguistic services
- IT services
- residential and commercial audiovisual
- personal and commercial insurance

If your industry is on this list, this book is for you. If your industry is not on this list, but an industry parallel to yours is, this book is for you. If neither of these statements apply, this book is still for you because this process has succeeded with over forty different industries and will succeed for you as well.

While reading this book, you will probably notice that you are already doing a few steps all the time and other steps some of the time. Some steps you may have never done before, either because you have never thought of it or because it is not the way you would prefer to buy. If a step would not represent your preferred way to buy, rather than disregarding it, I urge you to have curiosity and amusement, realizing that's just what makes your purchasing style unique. Realize that, for the specific step, your preferences are outside of the majority. It is rare that one person falls into the majority in all categories of anything. For instance, if I was to list the American favorite in different food categories, it would be likely, if you are American, that you would agree with the most popular choice most of the time but fall outside the favorite some of the time. Let's test it:

- American's favorite fruit: bananas
- American's favorite breakfast food: eggs
- American's favorite vegetable: broccoli
- American's favorite ice cream flavor: chocolate
- American's favorite pizza: pepperoni

How did you stack up? Did you align with all the food choices or just some of them? If you were hosting a group of Americans at an event, you would make sure eggs and bananas were served at breakfast, have more pepperoni pizza than any other type at lunch, have broccoli as a side vegetable, and, if you were offering ice cream for dessert, offer chocolate. With these selections, you would know that virtually everyone would be satisfied. You would choose that way even if you would prefer blueberry pancakes for breakfast, cheese pizza, and strawberry ice cream. Hosts take care of their guest's needs and wants, not their own. Such is the same in sales; using these steps is your way to best serve and take care of your prospects. It will keep them coming back for more.

The sales process you are about to learn makes all other sales processes obsolete. It is time for you to stop winging it with every sale. An inconsistent sales process leads to inconsistent results, which leads to uncertainty in your sales forecast. Right now, you have just taken the first step to change that. Welcome to the Warrior Selling process.

CHAPTER 1

The Warrior Selling Philosophy

I BELIEVE THAT ALL teachers have a moral obligation to be transparent about the lens through which they see the world. This allows students or readers to make informed decisions about whether they want to adopt the teacher's beliefs or strategies for themselves.

I remember reading a book in which the author wasn't up-front with his belief system, and the entire time I kept thinking, *Wow, this guy hates salespeople!* He stressed building a sales department so that salespeople couldn't take advantage of the company or client because his lens seemed to be that if given the opportunity that's exactly what salespeople would do! Had I known up front that he presupposed that salespeople were bad and manipulative, I would have made the informed decision not to read that book.

So be aware that I believe sales is a noble profession. I revere sales. I revere Sales Warriors. Sales Warriors are the ones who could take a salaried, nine-to-five job but choose instead to gamble on themselves. They know if they earn millions or go broke, it's on them. That is the Sales Warrior spirit that inspired me to dedicate my life to helping them succeed.

Every step in this book is written from the belief that not only is sales noble but salespeople are as well; furthermore, I believe this process will be used with the highest integrity. I believe that salespeople are good and that they choose to sell products or services that improve the world.

One of the questions I'm asked the most, and one that you are probably asking yourself right now is, "What is a Sales Warrior?" Let's start with what it means to be a warrior. Everyone has warrior moments; some just choose to have more of them. If you were a student who flunked a test, used that as motivation, and got an A in that class, that was a warrior moment. If you racked up debt and overcame it, have given birth, had a difficult conversation with your child, have fought against sickness or disease, have stood up to bullies, or have had to pick yourself up after a tough loss, those were warrior moments. A warrior that needs to be recognized and unleashed is already within you.

In all these Warrior moments, the roles of Servant, Leader, and Protector converge. For example, a parent serves the child by getting him or her to soccer and dance practice. That same parent will lead their child by teaching successful study habits to do well in school. That parent protects their child from the bullies and negative influences.

What does it mean to be a Sales Warrior? How do we apply our inner warrior to our roles as salespeople?

Sales Warriors are always leading, protecting, and serving. They lead their customers toward life improvement and away from pain. They protect their customers

from manipulation by the competition, or from other people in their life that don't have the knowledge that they do. They serve by helping their prospects discover their desires, dreams, and destiny while taking care of them, so the buying process isn't filled with fears, frustrations, and the failure of not finding a solution. Sales Warriors show their prospects why they need their product or service and highlight the consequence of not moving forward today.

To be the ultimate Sales Warrior, all three archetypes need to be present in all your customer interactions. Balancing the three archetypes makes the Sales Warrior.

Let's look at each of the archetypes on their own. Each one starts out good, with solid purpose and integrity, but if it becomes unbalanced and overgrown, the archetype becomes cancerous to the process and a shadow version of itself.

If someone only has the archetype of a Leader, it transforms into its shadow version, the Dictator. The Dictator is overly focused on the process and extremely rigid on having the prospect follow them, regardless of what is best for the prospect.

If someone only has the archetype of a Protector, it transforms into its shadow version, the Jail Warden. The Jail Warden is overly dogmatic, and though the person will be able to keep the prospect from going with competition, he or she could do so at the expense of what is best for the prospect.

If someone only has the archetype of a Servant, it transforms into its shadow version, the Pushover. The

Pushover will empathize and understand the prospect but get stuck in the sales version of the friend zone. The Pushover knows exactly what is best for the client but can't influence the client to act on what is best.

Now let's look at what happens if you have two strong archetypes and one that is underdeveloped. As you read them, think through your own relationships with prospects to determine which archetype you want to focus on engaging.

If you are a strong Leader and Protector but lack as a Servant, you will not understand your customers' deeper needs and risk losing rapport. Or worse, you won't deeply understand and empathize with them, and you could lead them to a product that wasn't the best option.

If you are a strong Protector and Servant, but lack as a Leader, you don't give your customers the bold advice and guidance they need to make decisions. You will be a kind salesperson who follows up, one who truly understands what solution your prospects need. But when they say they want time to think things over, you yield and allow them to make a huge purchasing decision without you.

If you are a strong Leader and Servant but lack in being a Protector, you are great at handling objections and guiding prospects to clarify their goals. You are also great at knowing what solution will help them attain their goals. But, without the protector side, you will forget to arm them with information and education that will protect them from the objections given by the news, their colleagues who haven't done any research, and the competition who will leave out important information.

To truly serve as a Sales Warrior and embody all the archetypes, you will also be known as a Benevolent Alpha, caring about the person and the outcome and having the courage to lead the way, be provocative, and speak the truth. It's the convergence of these three archetypes.

Beginning now, choose to fulfill your mission to lead, protect, and serve. Choose your higher purpose of being a Sales Warrior, something you were called to become. The moment you choose a career in sales, you choose a life of leading, protecting, and serving. Sales Warriors know that they are improving the lives of those they serve and earn what they are truly worth for doing it. The Sales Warrior believes sales isn't just a career; it's a *mission*.

The Warrior Selling process was created for all salespeople, but only Sales Warriors will succeed at the highest level. Some of the concepts in this book may feel uncomfortable to you at first, but that's the way of the warrior. Every great warrior is fighting a war—not against customers but is against their competition, their prospect's fears and insecurities about making big financial purchases, and their prospect's worry over not being taken care of and worry that purchasing is difficult. Your daily mission is convincing every prospect you speak to that the biggest mistake is not moving forward with you today. That is the identity of a Sales Warrior.

What is the Sales Warrior's philosophy? Everyone lives by a philosophy. Consciously or subconsciously, you have a philosophy about being a parent, spouse, and friend; about your health; and about your spirituality. The Warrior Selling philosophy is your philosophy for your career in sales and was created as your guiding focus through every sale, to constantly call back on, to keep you aligned with your mission and goals as a Sales Warrior. That philosophy is this:

> *"All human beings move away from pain and toward life improvement,* ***and a Sales Warrior believes their mission is to liberate them from any indecision."***

Whatever decisions you make, you are always either moving away from pain or trying to move toward some life improvement. Maybe you sell to consumers, with the purchase bringing more happiness or fulfillment in their personal life. Maybe you sell to other businesses, with purchases bringing more speed and profitability for the company. Whatever company or industry you are in, the effect is the same: the lives of your customers are improved by moving forward with you.

Let's look at the second part of our philosophy: Sales Warriors believe their mission is to liberate their customers from any indecision. I believe that nothing is more crippling for sales than ambiguity. I also believe the number one driving force of the human race is freedom from whatever is holding someone back from life improvement. In other words, people feel terrible when they don't know what to do, which product to buy, or which service will really get them to their goal. And the one motivator that pushes people to decide and "unstuck" themselves is freedom.

Humans are constantly in search of more freedom, even when it comes to the small, seemingly unimportant decisions in their life. For instance, why is it that whenever you drive home from work, you turn on the GPS to find the fastest route? Because you want freedom—from the traffic jam and your tough workday. After a long day of work, you are looking forward to your kids' 8:00 bedtime and a nice glass of wine with your spouse. Why? Because it is freedom from responsibilities.

In contrast, most other training companies will tell you that the philosophy of selling is to build long-term relationships. They believe that if you take your prospects to enough events and dinners or spend enough time building relationships, then eventually, they will buy from you. The "soft selling" revolution encouraged these untested and unfounded beliefs.

Let's examine some history. When the 1980s came, luxury and materialism were at their height. In 1984 the number-two hit on the US Billboard Hot 100 was—you guessed it—Madonna's "Material Girl." This culture was reflected in several hit sales movies, starting with *Wall Street* (1987), then *Glengarry Glen Ross* (1992), and even into the 2000s with *Wolf of Wall Street*, which was released in 2013 but took place in the 1980s. So, even thirty years later, we are still fascinated by the extremism of the eighties.

Most salespeople in the eighties were not corrupt as portrayed in these films, but a few were, and the media greatly amplified that. After this incredible level of improper salesmanship, the pendulum swung in the opposite direction. So instead of balancing out, we had the soft-selling revolution, which included books and training that were released in 1994 and 1998 by that name. Other soft-selling techniques that were popular were relationship selling and then consultative selling.

Such programs were not created to stand alone and be "the way" but instead were apologies for the behavior of the eighties. This swing to a softer side of selling is just as unhelpful and maybe even as hurtful as the other side. Now instead of people being manipulated quickly to make purchases that don't get them to their goal, salespeople are allowing prospects to walk away from life-improving solutions for fear of looking pushy. Just as many people are not getting the solutions they need.

I refuse to be a reaction to those before me. I will stand in the balance between caring about people and not allowing them to make the mistake of walking away from a solution that I *know* will improve their life. Some people think I am too hardcore or too pushy, but if a doctor knew of a medicine that would help me be healthier and didn't tell me because they were afraid of looking pushy, I would be pissed. So that is why I speak my truth and know I can sleep at night. I did what I was meant to do that day. The Sales Warriors I work with feel the same way. And together, all of us are leading the world to a new vision of what a salesperson is: a Warrior, leading, protecting, and serving. I am honored to invite you to join this mission with us.

The Warrior Selling philosophy is to provide what all customers desire at their core. They want to get away from their pain and move toward life improvement. They want a Sales Warrior who will liberate them from any ambiguity and indecision they feel during the buying process. This is not for the meek, and it will not give you permission for mediocrity. To succeed with this process, you must become the highest version of yourself. It's called Warrior Selling for a reason.

CHAPTER 2

The Warrior Selling Beliefs

'VE SPENT MY entire career using the Warrior Selling philosophy to ignite the pride, purpose, and respect for professional selling. From that philosophy came the fifteen foundational beliefs of the Sales Warrior, the core truths every Sales Warrior lives by, which form the backbone of every single tactic and mental-toughness technique you'll find in this book. In order to execute each of the twelve steps of this process with the right intention, you must understand the values. I start our training program with these beliefs because I only want to teach this process to people who will use it for the greater good.

Hold these beliefs as your guiding principles as you learn the Warrior Selling process. Every single step in this book stems from one of these beliefs, and every one of these beliefs connects to a step in the Warrior Selling process. This is your preworkout playlist to get you energized for the hard work ahead. These beliefs are your Sales Warrior anthem. Everything you are about to learn is with the assumption that you are ethical in selling something that improves the world and will use these techniques to make the world better.

Selling Means to Give Certainty plus Education with Rapport

Selling is more than influencing another to produce a mutually beneficial outcome. You can influence a buyer's thoughts, emotions, motivations, behaviors, and words. How you influence another can be broken down into certainty plus education with rapport.

Let's understand each part of the equation. The dictionary definition of certainty is "a firm conviction that something is the case." "When certainty is lost, all is lost" often echoes through the halls of FPG. This is because we constantly remind ourselves that it is of utmost importance to deliver certainty to our prospects. Consider these examples:

- When you become uncertain about your job, you quit.

- When your employer becomes uncertain about your attitude or abilities, you get fired.
- When prospects are uncertain about the economy, their finances, or what you are selling, they don't buy.
- When clients become uncertain about you or your company's ability to follow through on your brand promise, they cancel.

Certainty is everything. Certainty is your prospect's belief that your product is the solution that will work. Certainty leads to safety and security. When you can give your prospects certainty, you give them freedom. You give them life improvement. You need to make your prospects feel safe to buy from you, and the only way you can do that is to give them ultimate certainty in their decision to choose you over everyone else.

The next part of the equation is education, or constantly teaching your prospects something new. Educating your buyers is not new. But a side effect of education may not be understood: When you learn something new, no matter what it is, dopamine is released into your brain. It's a reward chemical that gives you that aha moment, and it is really satisfying. Dopamine also helps people to think, plan, and focus. So, educating your prospects doesn't just give them the knowledge to move forward, but it also begins to get them emotionally ready to make a big purchase with you.

The final piece of this belief is rapport, or being on the same page with someone. In order to have rapport, you must know what the prospect is trying to accomplish and be on a mission to help find that solution. When I first ask sales people—who may be influenced by soft selling—how they establish rapport, they often say something like, "Jason, rapport is whatever I have in common with my prospect" or "I get rapport by talking about their kids' sports or the same college we attended." Nope. That is not rapport—that is small talk. Small talk is not only unhelpful in moving a sale forward but also can actually hurt your sale. Remember, the prospect is talking to you because of a need for a product or service, not a need for a friend.

When I once worked with a sales team in Phoenix, someone in the room told me that in their CRM was a place to write the name of their prospects' grandmother. Their leadership said that in order to get people to trust them, they must get to know their family story. I wish I was making this up. Giving them permission to stick to the sales process and only talk about their prospects, families, or weekend plans if the prospect brought it up allowed them to work more efficiently, decreasing their sales conversion time by two meetings.

True rapport is understanding the prospect's immediate wants and what they are trying to achieve. Then it's about aligning with that vision so you can guide them to complete life improvement and fulfill your mission to lead, protect, and serve.

The Rule of Selling Is to Make It Easy for People to Spend Money to Improve Their Lives

People work hard to earn money, and they don't want to work hard to spend it. It's important that we simplify our buying process for our customers. Every customer is constantly in search of life improvement, whether personal or professional. That is achieved only if you can remove all the barriers keeping people from buying.

I ask all team members I work with if, having met with each of them today for the first time, I said yes to everything asked, how long would it take me to purchase? Depending on the industry, the interval would change, but none is fast enough. Today, people expect to be able to buy immediately, and more often than not, the prospect doesn't slow down the sale—the salesperson or their process does. So, think through to yourself, *How long does it take me to prepare a presentation, proposal, cost estimate, or project timeline? Is it easy for people to sign the contract? How about paying?* These all can be obstacles in the sale. I have been known to have my team chant, "Time kills deals" to have them remember to make it as easy as possible for the prospect to say yes, sign, and pay.

Now, you, the Sales Warrior in training, might not be the decision-maker for all the questions you just asked, but the point is that you can control how many options you give prospects; giving too many is one of the biggest sales slowing moves salespeople can make. More than three options cause decision fatigue, and the prospect becomes paralyzed. On the other hand, equally as harmful is only giving one option. With only one, the prospect can't help but wonder what other options exist. If you aren't showing them, then they will go to your competitors for it. Here's another saying: "One option is no option. Two options is a choice. And three options is *freedom*!" Make it easy for prospects to buy by giving them three options to choose from.

The Purpose of Selling Is to Convince the Just-Looking Buyer to Buy from You Today Over All Alternatives

Do you have prospects that are truly just looking, ones who are not ready, willing, and able to buy? Good! It is your job to get them ready, willing, and able. If every sale was easy, you would be on a salary, and I would be out of a job.

Some people first get turned off by the word *today* in the belief. What if the prospect wants to purchase next quarter?

Today is crucial: Why should people wait a single day to improve their life? If you have a way for them to have happier, easier days; be more productive; and increase their revenue, why should they wait? When you believe so strongly in improving your prospects' life and something you sell can do that, then you will treat every single conversation as if it is the last time you'll ever see the prospect in your life. You will leave it all on the field.

This belief programs you to think in urgent terms. Think, *How can I close this prospect today, right now?* Not every prospect will buy from you today; the point is that you are removing any rules about selling immediately being too soon. This belief gives you freedom from hesitation and shortens the process.

Now the "over all alternatives" part is pretty clear. Choosing you means prospects don't choose one of your competitors. It also means that they are not staying the course. And in order to help them choose you, you must discuss their other options. You must ask who else they are talking to and, if they don't move forward with you, what they are going to do. But, we will get into the exact way to bring up the competition in Step 2. For right now, just know that it is better for them to compare all of their options with you rather than without you.

The Objective of Selling Is to Make People Feel Wanted and to Achieve Resolution

If you make people feel *big*, they will buy *big*. If you make them feel small, they buy small. It's that simple. By asking your customers to buy, you are making them feel wanted. You are subconsciously telling them that what you are selling was created specifically with them in mind and that they belong. You are saying, "I choose you to be our next customer. Will you accept?"

The second part of the objective of selling is to achieve resolution. Notice that I didn't say to "close" the sale. Your product or service is not for everyone, and if you have been in sales for any time at all, you have probably sold to someone you wished you hadn't. Never leave people in ambiguity; help them achieve resolution, whether with you, with a competitor, or with whatever they are currently doing. Being the one who leads them to this resolution is part of being the trusted advisor in your industry.

Selling Is about Getting the Customer to Buy Sooner and for More Money than Originally Planned

Are you feeling weird about this one? Let me explain. I am frequently asked, "Is it unethical to have to convince people to spend more money than they were planning?" Only if the amount is more than they could afford. Customers have a certain idea of what they believe something's going to cost, and most customers don't realize what the actual price of something is. Your job is to figure out what problem they are trying to solve and what life improvements they are trying to gain and to present your solutions.

Buying sooner means they don't have to keep putting off that life improvement. The reason they won't buy today is that they don't fully understand how it is going to improve their life. So educate them. Help them feel good, that they are in alignment with the money they are spending and the sped-up time frame.

The Sales Warrior Is the Primary Source of Confidence, Motivation, Hope, and Certainty in the Prospect's Decision

Outside voices are influencing your prospects all the time. They have many different people with many different opinions telling them how to spend their money and what to spend it on. Maybe their friends tell them to choose someone else's brand instead of yours. Maybe their boss or their board tells them that now really isn't a good time to buy anything because it's outside the budget. Maybe the news they watch every morning carries the same message—the economy is crashing, the world is over, time to hunker down and not buy anything. It's a constant onslaught that prospects are not prepared to handle without a Sales Warrior. They become overwhelmed because they are not prepared to handle all of these external objections. Always remember, you are the expert in your field, not the other outside voices, so speak confidently and make sure you are balancing the amount of uncertainty the world is giving them by giving and portraying more certainty.

The Sales Warrior is the chosen one who can provide freedom and liberation from all outside voices. You know how to provide confidence in your leadership. You know how to provide motivation to move forward in the sale. You know how to provide hope in what you are selling them. You know how to provide certainty that they have made the right choice by going with you. No one in your prospect's life knows your business, product, or service the way you do, and it is your responsibility to be the primary source of confidence, motivation, hope, and certainty for your prospect.

Resolution Comes by Balancing Speed and Flexibility

Sales success is not just measured by conversion rate. Conversion time is equally important. You can still go broke if you have a 100 percent conversion rate but you take twelve months to close a deal. Speed is important and something you should be tracking for yourself. When someone needs you right now, they are urgent to get your product; speed is obvious. But what about when a prospect isn't in dire need. How is speed necessary then?

I think of it this way: A great salesperson is like a really effective doctor. When the prospect is "sick," that person is locked in a state of ambiguity or stress. Your job as the Sales Warrior is to diagnose that sickness and convince the prospect to take the medicine you are prescribing to get better. If the patient isn't sick yet, it's the Sales Warrior's job to help the patient fully realize that with no change in habits, sickness is right around the corner. Your speed is now to help them put a preventative plan together and act quickly.

The biggest resource your prospects have isn't their money—it's their time. And guess what? Yours is too. The shorter you can shrink your conversion time, the more time you have to close more prospects and lead them to life improvement. You need to be able to speak as efficiently and effectively as possible.

Flexibility comes from listening to the wants, needs, and concerns of every prospect. Your flexibility is your creativity, the way you can bend your process and style for the prospect in front of you. How can you accommodate the individual's uniqueness? What can you do in your presentation that is specific to the prospect? Can you blend your offerings to more exactly match what is needed? In great art of all kinds, there is first a science, be it painting, sculpture, music, or dance. Only after that science is mastered can the artist claim ownership in a beautiful way that speaks to the soul of the viewer. The same is true for sales. Your sales process is your science, your speed. Your flexibility is your art—how you make it yours and how you connect with the individual in front of you.

All Customers Have Hidden and Admitted Needs; the Sales Warrior Must Solve Both

The customers have admitted a problem in need of a solution, but they also have the problem behind the problem. They have needs behind their needs. For a consumer purchase, the admitted need is that they need a home with an extra bedroom for their growing family. The hidden need is to alleviate the fighting because of being on top of each other all the time. On the business side, the admitted need is that they need a new website for their company. Their hidden need is that they currently don't have enough leads coming in for the sales team to hit their goals. The Sales Warrior must solve both needs, not just what customers want and think they need but also the problems they didn't even know they had with solutions they didn't even know they needed.

I love when a great Sales Warrior comes into my life. In summer of 2010, in Fort Worth, Texas, I was in the market for a new car. That summer had one hundred days over 100 degrees. It was a scorcher. I went to the Land Rover dealership and gave them my specs: year, color, and so forth. And within ten minutes, we were out on a test drive. That's when I got a weird sensation in my seat area—not weird bad, but different. I looked at my passenger, the Sales Warrior; he smiled and asked how I liked the cooling seats. Cooling seats? I had no idea these existed. I left the dealership with a new car, spending more than I had planned, with upgrades that hours earlier I hadn't known existed. I had a hidden need—a cool bottom. Thank goodness the Sales Warrior didn't listen to exactly what I asked for and give me that!

The Most Important Aspects of Selling are How Fast You Can Get the Position of Strength, and Whether or Not You Can Keep It

Your position of strength is nothing more than the reason your prospects are talking to you. It can be what they like about what you are selling, what they heard about your brand, how they got interested in it, or why they got interested. Those are the vital pieces of information you can use to lead the sale. Position of strength is so important for three reasons:

- You get to determine the price and the terms of the sale rather than does the prospect.

- The prospect has certainty in you as the advisor.
- The prospect is invested emotionally rather than logically because he or she feels connected to you and what you are selling.

It's important to be in a position of strength, but it's even more important to establish it in the opening minutes of speaking to your prospect.

This may be the first time you have heard the term *position of strength*, but you know what it feels like when the position of strength changes hands. If you are giving a great selling presentation and your prospect tells you, "Wow, I had no idea this existed!" you have a position of strength. When a prospect says, "Look, I'm just not sure this is right for us," that means you have lost your position of strength. The Sales Warrior knows position of strength is gained within the first few minutes of the interaction and must work to keep it all the way to the close. We will discuss exactly how to gain a position of strength in Step 1 of the process.

Performance Equals Knowledge Minus Leashes

I believe all achievement in your life boils down to one simple-to-understand formula.

PERFORMANCE = Knowledge - Leashes

Your performance is your sales results—either how many units you sell or how much revenue you bring in. Those results are equal to your knowledge: company knowledge, product knowledge, industry knowledge, financing knowledge, sales process knowledge, and so forth, minus any leashes you have. The leashes are the head trash that keeps you from acting on your knowledge.

For instance, if you know to follow up with prospects but hesitate because a voice in your head says, "They are probably busy right now, and you will be interrupting" or "People don't like to be contacted by phone, so probably you should just send a text," then you are leashed. We all have leashes; what is important is to identify them so you can get rid of them and act on all your knowledge. This is the answer to the mystery of why a new salesperson can join a team, know basically nothing about the industry, and start outselling the sales veterans who have been there for years. Check out the following formulas. This veteran is a ten out of ten on knowledge, but with an eight on leashes the performance is only a two. The leashes might be something like, "You need to have at least four conversations with someone before you ask for

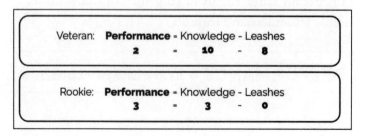

the sale" or "Only follow up three times; after that you look like a pushy sales guy." Those leashes make all the knowledge irrelevant, and this salesperson only sells two units a month. All the while, our rookie, who only has a three on knowledge, has none of those leashes (leashes come from experience), and so is able to sell three units that month, outselling the veteran who knows so much more. The goal, of course, is to have a ten on knowledge and a 0 on leashes. And this is possible, with awareness and discipline.

I've published an entire book dedicated to this formula alone. The book you are reading now is the process piece. The mindset piece of Warrior Selling is in my book *Stop Your Sales Fear: 42 Strategies to Remove the Self-Image, Stories, Reluctances, and Rules That are Holding You Back.*

All you need to know right now for this book is that there are four types of knowledge that you need to acquire to remove any leashes you may have:

- Brand: Your brand messaging is what makes your company unique and unrivaled. It's vital that you don't just know that branding; you must own it to truly sell it.
- Product: The products or services, features, and benefits you sell are what give your company its unique selling position. Your success and the success of your company often depend on how

KNOWLEDGE

PRODUCT: The products, features, and benefits you sell are what give your company the unique selling position it currently occupies. Your success and the success of your company often depends on how well you can sell your products based upon the knowledge you possess.

SELLING SKILLS: Your process and language. The most effective selling is 80% process-driven science and 20% individual art. That means having a defined, science-based process and most effective words that allow you to sell to any prospect, in any situation.

BRAND: Your brand messaging is what makes you unique and unrivaled as a company. It's vital that you don't just know that branding; you must own it to truly sell it.

FINANCE: Top Sales Warriors know the financial side of their products inside and out. You can comfortably and simply explain the financing and payment plan options as well as the benefits and the return on investment your prospects will get when they purchase with you.

well you can sell your products based upon the knowledge you possess.

- Finance: Top Sales Warriors know the financial side of their products inside and out. You can comfortably and simply explain the financing and payment plan options as well as the benefits and the return on investment your prospects will get when they purchase with you.
- Selling Skills: This includes your process and language. The most effective selling is 80 percent process-driven science and 20 percent individual art. That means having a defined, science-based process and the most effective words that allow you to sell to any prospect, in any situation. This book is dedicated to teaching you this type of knowledge.

That is your knowledge, but if you want maximum performance, it's more than just knowing something. You must remove your leashes.

Here are four types of leashes you are fighting every day:

- Self-image: Your self-image represents your internal beliefs about yourself and your capabilities. For example, self-image leashes may be "I'm not worthy of earning a six-figure income," or "I don't identify as a Sales Warrior."

LEASHES

Stories: A story is an assumption based on external circumstances that may or may not be true. For example, "people don't buy my product in a down economy."

Rules: Rules are what you need to see, feel, or hear in order to have permission to engage with your prospect. For example, "I never ask for the close until at least the third conversation."

Self-Image: Your self-image represents your internal beliefs about yourself and your capabilities. For example, "I'm not worthy of earning a six-figure income."

Reluctances: A reluctance is a fear of selling in a certain situation or to a certain type of person. For example, a fear of closing sales over the phone or a fear of selling to a high net worth individual.

- Stories: A story is an assumption, based on external circumstances, that only might be true. An assumption leash could be, for example, "People don't buy my product or service in a down economy" or "If my company has another price increase, then I will lose many of my prospects, causing me to miss my forecast."
- Reluctances: A reluctance is a fear of selling in a certain situation or to a certain type of person. For example, you may say, "I am stronger at closing someone face to face versus over the phone or using Zoom" or "If I ask someone to purchase too soon, then I risk turning the customer off and losing the sale."
- Rules: Rules are what you need to see, feel, or hear to have permission to engage with your prospect. For example, a leash might be "I never ask for the close until at least the third conversation" or "I know that when the prospect smiles, I am getting a buying signal."

The performance you achieve daily is equal to the amount of knowledge you have minus the number of leashes you have. Given the equation, true Sales Warriors are constantly focused on adding knowledge and removing leashes. The quest is never-ending.

Objections Are within the Customer, Not Between the Customer and You

Imagine a teenager and a parent talking over college options. The teen is struggling with his college choice, frustrated because he can't figure out the right one. A tense back and forth occurs between the parent and son because of much built-up confusion and ambiguity.

An observer might think that the parent and child are fighting. But the parent doesn't take the situation personally; it's not about the parent at all. The raised voice and intense emotions are an internal conversation the teenager is having with himself. The parent thus doesn't respond with the same frustration, anger, and confusion but instead responds with certainty, guidance, and care. The parent can handle the worries and concerns because they know that none of it is personal, it's not an attack, and it's not about them; it's about the child being frustrated in not knowing which direction to go.

The same is true when you are with prospects. The objections they give you are just their internal conversation. It's not about you, and your job as a Sales Warrior is to guide them through the internal struggle and lead them to what they are trying to achieve: life improvement.

This is a powerful and liberating belief for Sales Warriors. If it's not about you, then everything is working in your favor. Nothing is a fight or an attack or a struggle; what appears to be so is just a conversation you can help guide toward total resolution without a shred of fear.

The Sales Warrior Can Sell Anything by Breaking the Sale into Small Decisions.

You may think your customer is only making one decision, to buy or not. The reality is that many decisions need to be made before the final decision. This process can be overwhelming because you need to convince the customer to make the overall decision to buy from you. Top Sales Warriors know that decisions that must be made before someone can buy from you. Microdecisions could be the following:

- "Am I unsatisfied with my current product or service?"
- "Is this new product or service better than what I currently have?"
- "Is this product or service better than the alternatives?"
- "Do I feel certain that the brand is going to follow through on its commitments?"
- "Based on the current economy, do I feel it is the right time to buy?"
- "Is this within my budget?"

I believe a customer will answer such questions with or without you, so if you can break down all decisions into bite-size chunks, you can take away any pain the customer experiences and lead him or her to life improvement faster.

The *Why* Must Be Greater than the Sacrifice

Harvard Business Review conducted a study that showed 95 percent of all purchasing decisions happen emotionally, not logically.[3] That means that they happen on the subconscious level uncontrolled by the logical part of their brain. We are genetically wired to make decisions emotionally, whether buying for ourselves or for our business. The *why* is everything.

Every purchase involves some kind of sacrifice on the customer's part, such as the price, product, time commitment, personal or company disruption, not having family or coworker approval, or any number of factors. Whatever that sacrifice is, their *why* must be greater. That reason is the cure, the emotional urgency, the emotional connection. It's your job as a Sales Warrior to demonstrate that life improvement and that the value of what you are selling is worth whatever sacrifice they will make. If the sacrifice is greater, there will be no sale.

A Warrior Sale Must Involve Conflict, Compromise, and Collaboration and Challenge Perspective

I want you to think about one of the more challenging sales you have made. Chances are, the buyer had several big objections, and with each one, you had to help the person see the bigger picture and change the perspective. The buyer probably also wanted all the bells and whistles you offer at the price of your base product. Because of that, you had to help the prospect compromise on features, price, or both.

In my experience, those prospects became my absolute best clients, my most loyal clients who stayed with me for years because I *worked* for the sale. It wasn't just handed to me; it was a Warrior sale. It was as if we went through a battle together and came out the other side on the same team, which left us with incredibly strong rapport.

A market sale is when your prospect comes to you already convinced to buy, and you are there to facilitate the transaction. The time of purchase is socially acceptable for what you are selling. A Warrior sale is when the prospect comes to you and is not convinced yet. Market sales do not seduce Sales Warriors; Warriors embrace the productive conflict that brings resolution. They know that true resolution can't possibly happen without productive conflict. They constantly challenge their prospects' perspectives about something they believed to be true that held them back from buying.

For example, a business owner says, "In a down economy, we can't invest in training," versus, "Training will upgrade our skills and give us the advantage we need in an uncertain economy." The Sales Warrior helps the owner believe the latter. The warrior forces compromise and gets their prospects to see that there are no unicorn products or services. They collaborate with their prospects all along the way to keep that steady rapport throughout the sale. You don't grow your business year over with market sales; you do it with Warrior sales.

Being a Sales Warrior involves being proactive versus reactive. It's about acting versus letting the world decide for you, about seizing the opportunity in front of you. I love this quote from former President Harry Truman:

> "People make history, not the other way around. In periods where there is no leadership, society stands still. Progress occurs when courageous, skillful leaders seize the opportunity to change things for the better."

You are in charge of your own destiny as a Sales Warrior. You will not earn more by waiting for market sales to fall in your lap. You earn more when you take the path of a Sales Warrior and make every sale a Warrior sale.

The Coaching Makes All the Difference

Sales Warriors don't just want coaching or ask for coaching—they demand it. No great athlete ever said, "You know what, I've got this all figured out. I don't need coaching. I'll take it from here." All people with drive know that to get to the next level, they need a coach. If you could do it alone, you would have done it alone by now. It doesn't matter how good you are; a great coach will always push you to the next level.

Your level of improvement is a direct result of your desire for coaching.

CHAPTER 3

The Warrior Selling Process: Overview

I BELIEVE THAT LIFE is nothing more than a series of decisions. No matter how small decisions seem at the time, the accumulation of every single one makes you into the person you are today.

Selling is the same—it's about leading the customer to decide to choose you during every step of the sale. It's about giving your customers absolute certainty that you can improve their life better than anyone else.

Warrior Selling is a twelve-step process to convert a sale. The first five steps are to understand your customer's mission. The next four steps are to present solutions. And the final three are to resolve the sale. Our clients have liked calling this the 5/4/3 Factor.

Think about the last time you had to assemble a new piece of furniture—maybe it was a bookcase, a crib, or a dresser. You opened the box and took out all the different pieces and screws and bolts. What is the first thing you did? You reviewed the instructions and the step-by-step guide. Did you think you would be able to complete the setup without them? Maybe you could have, but it would have taken you a lot longer, you'd have quite a few setbacks, and you'd experience a lot of frustration. You'd be staring at all these pieces scattered across the floor, wondering how it's going to become this beautiful image on the front of the box. Luckily, when you have a guide, you can chunk it down, step-by-step, so that you can feel confident with the outcome.

The same goes for your selling process: you can sell *anything* by breaking it down into small decisions for your customers. That's why The Warrior Selling 5/4/3 Factor was created: to chunk down those decisions to a minute-by-minute process so you can sell to anyone, in any industry, in any circumstance.

Let's go through each stage so you can see how it all fits together.

The Five Steps to Understand the Customer's Mission
First, you must understand why this prospect is searching and what brought the prospect to you. Next, understand

their goals, objectives, and outcome frames. Before you present your solutions, you must be on the same page as your prospect and have a firm grasp of the desired outcome versus. the current situation, along with the other alternatives under consideration. That's how you get that position of strength right away.

1. The Four Steps to Present Solutions

The goal in this stage is to take the problems you discovered in the first stage and present your solutions. In this stage, you learn how to provide more certainty and keep that sale moving forward by demonstrating your features and benefits. You highlight the advantages of your product over the status quo and over what your competitors have. You use the five steps to understand why your prospect isn't happy with the current situation. Then you use the four steps to present solutions for that problem by showing the prospect why and how you can offer the best product or service to achieve the outcome. And you do all of this while handling any objections.

2. The Three Steps to Resolve the Sale

Selling is about resolution, and this stage is where you extract anything that's keeping the buyer from having that resolution and give certainty so the prospect can buy from you today. We don't call these the three steps to *close* the sale because the *close* is a result of the resolution. This stage involves removing any ambiguity and replacing it with certainty.

Now that you have all the foundational knowledge you need to be successful with this process, let's dive into the twelve steps of the Warrior Selling process so you can start achieving a 100 percent conversion rate.

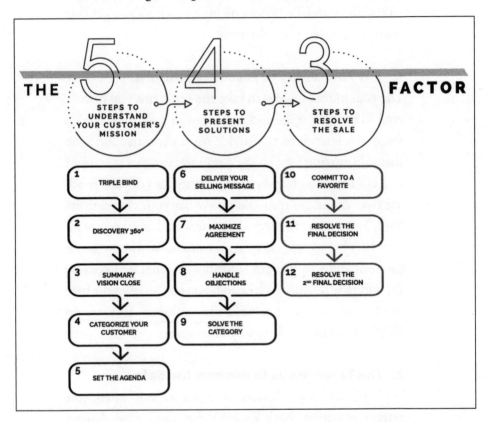

CHAPTER 4

Is a Question Just a Question?

THROUGHOUT THIS PROCESS, you are going to be doing three things: asking questions, listening to understand, and educating. Before I teach you the process, which is how to educate, I will discuss different question types and when to use each. The twelve steps will refer back to them.

Why would you ask questions? The purpose is to uncover the following:

- Admitted and hidden problems that your customer has

- The customer's desire to improve his or her life
- The advantages and disadvantages of the current solution
- The alternative solutions under consideration
- Any areas of resistance, which give you a position of strength

The purpose of asking questions is not for any of these reasons:

- To see what you both have in common
- To get to know the buyer personally
- To find out what the prospect is doing this weekend

Unless you are a mind reader, the only way to find out what people are thinking is to ask them. You may not realize that *how* you ask questions of your customer will determine how strong your position of strength will be right away. Don't ask someone a close-ended question, otherwise known as a yes-or-no question. Instead, ask open-ended questions, like "How can I help you?" For as long as I have been in sales, I have been taught this way.

Yes-no answers give some information but not any details. Wanting more and better information led to using open-ended questions in sales. The prospect has the opportunity to give us the specifics. That was a great intention, but it didn't work out the exact way it was expected to. Unfortunately, people don't like limitless options; it makes their brains work too hard, so the actual effect was a universal human auto-response to all sales questions: "I'm just looking."

The science behind why humans don't like or respond to the open-ended question is that it creates anxiety in the brain. This is called the paradox of choice. The more options you give someone, the more the brain becomes overwhelmed and shuts down. Studies also show that the fewer choices you give someone, the more likely that person is to decide. If you give someone three options, they are more scientifically likely to pick one than if you gave them six, ten, twenty, or an infinite amount. What followed was the next evolution of the opening question: the Triple Bind, a fancy name for a multiple-choice question.

When my wife and I are wrapping up our workday and I ask her innocently, "What do you want to do for dinner?" what kind of response do you think I get? You guessed it: "I don't know, what do you want to do?" But here is what I do know: my wife and I eat dinner every night; we have lived in the same city for over twenty years, so we know the restaurants and what kind of food we like and don't like. But we still struggle to decide.

In contrast, imagine that I brilliantly ask her, "Honey, for dinner tonight would you like to go out for sushi, steaks, or pasta?" What kind of response do you think I will get? Yep, she can easily answer. (For the record, it will be sushi, so I never offer sushi unless that's what I want to eat that night!)

So, now imagine opening your conversation with a prospect by saying, "There are three main reasons that people want to do business with us—A, B, and C. Which interests you the most?" This is the easiest and fastest way to gain a position of strength with the prospect, who can easily answer your question, getting the sales momentum going.

In Step 1, the Triple Bind, I will give you a process to help you create a strong opening for your process. First, let's discuss two more types of questions that will be used in Step 2 and beyond: eliciting and installing questions.

Eliciting and installing are versions of open-ended questions and thus should be used later in a sales process after the momentum of the conversation has already been established—which is why they won't be explored until Step 2. Every question we ever ask either elicits an unfiltered response from the prospect or installs a direction we want the prospect to go. The key is to be conscious and purposeful of the kinds of questions you ask. First, you will need to understand what our desired outcome is. Then you can formulate a question to achieve that goal. The most successful Sales Warriors are master communicators and are intentional about when they install and when they elicit for their desired outcome.

Eliciting questions give you a blank canvas for your prospect to share opinions and express and elaborate on their feelings and emotions. They add color and enrichment to the prospect's beliefs about something. However, you must be strategic on when to do that. If you recklessly elicit a response, it can backfire because the prospect might say something that causes you to lose position of strength.

Here are some examples of eliciting questions:

- Tell me about your current situation.
- Tell me about your ideal solution.
- What is your vision for _____?
- Tell me about what made you decide to speak with me today.
- Tell me more about that.
- What do you mean by that?
- What does that look like for you?
- What causes you to feel that way?
- What is important to you about that?
- What would having that mean to you?
- What criteria are you using to make your decision?
- What is important to you when considering _____?

As you can see, these questions add more depth to a topic already being discussed and make sure that you are in rapport (or on the same page) with the prospect. When you ask eliciting questions, you are in the Servant archetype, because you sincerely want to understand what the prospect experiences.

Installing questions allow you to guide the conversation by giving a clue within the question to the type of answer you are looking for. For instance, you could ask your prospect, "What do you like best about what I have shared with you today?" You have just installed that the prospect likes what you have shared, and you guide him or her to verbalize it for you. If I wanted to ask the same question but from an eliciting perspective, I would ask, "What do you think about what I have shared today?" The prospect can answer in any way, saying he or she liked it, loved it, hated it, or had no thoughts about it. With installation questions, you eliminate the types of answers you don't want so you can move the conversation along quicker and with more purpose.

You will either be in your Leader archetype or our Protector archetype when asking installing questions. Ask yourself, *In what direction do I want to guide my prospect? What do I want to hear from the prospect that will help that person move toward a resolution?*

Here are some examples of installation questions. I will underline where the installation is:

- What do you <u>like</u> about what you currently have? (I am installing that the prospect likes something.)
- What <u>don't you like</u> about what you currently have? (I am installing that the prospect doesn't like something.)
- What are the <u>alternatives</u> you are looking at? (I am installing that the prospect is looking at alternatives.)

- What does the <u>alternative not have</u> that is causing you to keep looking? (I am installing that the alternative is not a suitable option.)
- What are the <u>potential risks</u> of you not moving forward today? (I am installing that there are risks to not buying from me today.)
- What is the <u>perceived risk of moving forward</u> today? (I am installing that any risk is just perceived but not real.)
- How does having this _____ <u>solve your problem</u> of _____? (I am installing that buying my product will solve the prospect's problems.)

And here are a few examples of advanced installation questions for those of you ready:

- I know you said you are just looking, but that is what <u>my last customer said today, and that customer bought</u>. (I am installing that when people who are just looking buy during the first conversation.)
- How are you going to feel after <u>someone else purchased</u> your first choice? (I am installing that if the prospect doesn't purchase today, someone else will.)
- If <u>both</u> of us were <u>free</u>, then whom would you choose? (This one is my favorite. I am installing that if we removed the fees, the customer would choose me over the competition.)

Installation questions guide the prospect in making decisions. They also help you to uncover the hidden and admitted problems your customer has and allows you to understand his or her desire to improve in the fastest way possible.

That's why my approach is to use eliciting questions as a follow-up to installation questions.

Installation questions give permission to the prospect to share hidden fears, frustrations, and failures, in addition to desires and dreams, by guiding the person toward those answers. The answers increase your probability of controlling the outcome. Just like with eliciting questions, only use installation questions with something you know how to handle. For instance, if you install with the first example, "What do you like about what you currently have?" make sure that you know how to address whatever the answer may be. Know that you are going to listen and remember what was said, and when giving your presentation, you are going to show the prospect that your product has what was liked about the current product. Or if the prospect answers with something that you don't provide, know that your next step is to build enough value in what you do offer that you can handle that objection down the road.

As the ultimate Sales Warrior, be strategic about getting to your desired outcome with your prospects. Only ask questions that move the sale forward as efficiently and effectively as possible.

THE FIVE STEPS TO UNDERSTAND YOUR CUSTOMER'S MISSION

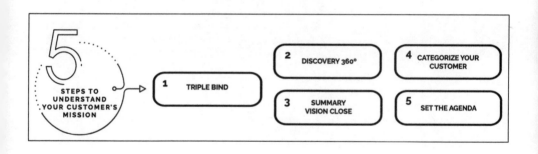

5 STEPS TO UNDERSTAND YOUR CUSTOMER'S MISSION

1 TRIPLE BIND

2 DISCOVERY 360°

3 SUMMARY VISION CLOSE

4 CATEGORIZE YOUR CUSTOMER

5 SET THE AGENDA

CHAPTER 5

Step 1:
The Triple Bind

The Triple Bind controls the conversation right at the opening of the process by leading the client to talk about the benefits you offer
                    —Nicholas, commercial real estate

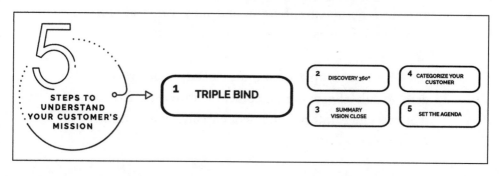

49

ENEFITS TO THE customer: Helps your customer feel big, so you start the process with a win.

Benefits to you: Gives you position of strength and gets the prospect in a decision-making rhythm from the start of the sale.

If I could show you a way to ask questions to prospects that could help them feel confident right away, tell you exactly what is most important to them, or position you to lead the conversation, which one would be the most interesting to you?

And right there, I have demonstrated our first step, the Triple Bind. Did you mentally answer the question? Was your answer one of the options I gave? Was it more than one option? Did you add in your own fourth option? All of those are great answers and will lead us into a discussion about you and your process. I win, and you win no matter what you choose. This step is simple but smart. If you feel good about it, you can skip down to the paragraph that begins with "Here's how to create your Triple Bind." If you want to nerd out on the science a bit more, then keep on reading.

Binding questions are easy for your customer to answer, create a position of strength, puts the customer in a decision-making rhythm, and moves the sale forward. And if you want to end the sale strong, you must start strong.

The first couple of minutes of the sales process dramatically affects the outcome. Neuroscience tells us that we judge information sequentially, which means that every human forms opinions and makes decisions based on the order in which they receive information. Everything builds on everything else, so your first impression forms the foundation for how you will perceive every bit of information with that person going forward. This makes it crucial for you to begin your relationship by taking the lead and making the prospect feel comfortable, as well as inviting him or her into a conversation the person wants to be a part of. Starting slow, on the other hand, drops you into a hole that is hard to crawl out of.

After I first switched to binding questions myself, and later teaching thousands of other sales professionals to do it, I realized that when Sales Warriors started strong, their probability of closing the sale went up dramatically. I also discovered that the overall time spent with the prospect was longer. The more you can understand your prospects by asking strategic questions, the more you can educate, the more objections you can handle, the more decisions you can resolve, and the more you increase your probability of winning the sale.

One of the beliefs of a Sales Warrior is that the most important thing in selling is position of strength—how fast you can get it and whether you can sustain it. The sales process is a constant tug-of-war over position of strength with your prospects.

One of my clients had a face-to-face appointment with a high-level executive who told her, "That was a great presentation; you made some great points." That may seem like a small moment in the middle of the sale, but that's what position of strength sounds like. A prospect of another of my clients told her, "I just don't see the value for the price." At that moment she lost position of strength. That's why establishing your position of strength before you do anything else is the key to the sale.

Here are the three benefits of having the position of strength up front:

- You will get to determine the price and the terms of the sale rather than the prospect doing so.
- Your prospect will have certainty in you as the advisor, which means the prospect will yield to you taking the lead.
- You get the prospect into a decision-making rhythm from the start of the sale.

So many salespeople start every conversation with an open-ended question: "Tell me what you are looking for," or "How can I help you?" Although these questions aren't wrong, they just are not the best way to open a conversation. Here are four reasons why open-ended questions are ineffective if used nonstrategically:

- It makes the prospect work to buy from you.
- It overwhelms your prospect with too many choices to consider.
- It gives the prospect the position of strength.

- It allows the prospect to take the leadership position and control the process.

Does this mean that you never ask open-ended questions? Of course not. But you only ask open-ended questions when it's easy for the customer to answer and their answer moves them closer to buying from you.

That's the psychology behind Triple Binds. You want to make it easier for the customers to engage with you and to find the solution or product that will improve their life the most. When you ask an open-ended question, you are putting all the pressure on the customers to know exactly what they are looking for. Open-ended questions like "How can I help you?" presuppose that every prospect you come in contact with already knows what they want—even though most prospects start in the just-looking stage and don't know what they want or need yet. Those customers will respond to open-ended questions with "I'm not sure." Basically, what they are saying is "When I see what I want, I'll ask for your help." Though they don't know what they want, they know what they *don't* want. And now they have the position of strength.

Starting the sales process with a binding question is game-changing for your sales because it puts you in the driver's seat. You are leading the way and giving your prospect certainty. Ambiguity triggers feelings of stress, and you are taking that stress away.

Let's go back to our end-of-the-day discussion on what to have for dinner. Is it typically easier to know what you do want or what you don't want? In this scenario, and most scenarios, most people are unsure what they want, but know with certainty what they *don't* want.

The same concept applies to your prospects. If you call on prospects or sell over the phone, then you know that many times people want a product, and, after hearing about why they are looking, you realize the product they need is not what they asked for. That, coupled with some customers only knowing what they don't want, means that guiding your customers from the very beginning of the process helps move things along more efficiently and effectively and with more certainty than yielding the sales process over to the prospect.

The Triple Bind makes people feel smart by starting the conversation with them having the correct answer. Remember, when people feel big, they buy big. If we give them three choices, and they have something different, they'll tell you. We want to protect them from saying "I don't know." Those words make them feel incompetent, and then they won't want to be around you anymore. We're removing that feeling by giving them three answers that will help them start the conversation feeling big.

Here's how to create your Triple Bind:

1. Write down the three most compelling reasons why someone buys from you. Maybe you are the industry leader in a certain category, or people choose you because you have the most value for what you offer. Make

sure you choose the three strongest reasons that will move the sale forward.

2. Only focus on things you offer, not things you don't offer. You want to positively reinforce your selling message, not negatively reinforce it.

3. Make sure that your compelling reasons are features you have that your competitors don't. Remember, your position of strength is ultimately about why prospects are unsatisfied with what they currently have or don't have.

4. Test it out with live prospects. You might pick your three compelling reasons, but in the real world, you find more relevant reasons that buyers choose you. This is where you can ask, "So what was the final reason why you decided to move forward with us?" Then you can pivot to using those things in the future because you have done the experiential study. Always keep your eyes and ears open to what your prospects are saying.

After you put everything together, your Triple Bind might sound something like this: "People choose us because of blank, blank, and blank. Of those three things, which is most relevant for what you are looking for?"

The Triple Bind needs to be delivered within the first ninety seconds of initial contact. You want your customer to see right away the compelling reasons people pick you.

What follows are three scenarios in which you could use the Triple Bind.

In-Person Retail Purchase

"Hi, Mr. Customer, my name is Jason. Welcome to XYZ company. There are a few reasons why people are interested in XYZ company: A, B, or C. I'm curious—what brought you in today?"

B2B Scheduled Appointment, First Encounter

"Hi, Mr. Customer, thanks for taking this meeting. I want to be respectful of your time, so I want to get right down to it. There are three reasons people do business with us: A, B, or C. Of those, what are you most interested in talking about today?"

Cold Call

"Hi, Mr. Customer, this is Jason Forrest with FPG. Thanks for taking my call. I see that you are currently hiring sales professionals. Is this correct?"

"Great! FPG has disrupted the recruiting industry by combining a sales head-hunting and sales training company in one. There are a few reasons why companies like yours are interested in outsourcing their sales recruiting needs. One, the candidates they are attracting are not strong enough. Two, companies haven't been able to attract any candidates. Or three, the people they have hired recently have failed to deliver. I'm curious, out of those three, what is your biggest problem right now?"

Using the Customer's Language

However you are delivering your Triple Bind, you want to make sure you use your customer's language. The Triple Bind of a team I worked with was too high-level. It was all about "quality," "durability," "high performance," "family-owned," "energy-efficient," "been around for thirty years," and so forth. I said, "Which of those things can your competitors also say?" and they said, "None of them!" And I said, "No, they can say all of them!"

There's nothing wrong with all of those things, but you need to look at if those are truly the reasons why someone is going to choose you over the competition. One of the ways you can craft your Triple Bind is to create a list of everything that you might put in it. What are the reasons why people choose to buy with you? What are the reasons why you would choose to buy? Then ask yourself, *Are we the best at this?*

You can be energy efficient or have quality, but are you really the *best*? Can you say confidently, "I have the highest-quality product out there," and back it up with evidence? Can any of your competitors mention this as well? You have to find the things on your list for which you are the *only* one. You also want to make sure to avoid buzzwords because they end up meaning nothing. In fact, Wendy's slogan is "Quality is Our Recipe," and Walmart's slogan is "Save Money, Live Better." So, you can see how "quality" is not a standard. And how exactly would you "live better" after a trip to Walmart?

One of the mistakes that people make when creating their Triple Binds is they use industry jargon. FPG was working with a big machine company whose Triple Bind included *durability*, but the customer had never asked for it. Instead, the customer said it was important that the machines didn't break down. Even though *durability* encompasses that idea, the customer wants to hear you use his or her language.

Use the language of the people you are speaking to. As salespeople, we want so badly to educate other people, to show everything that we've learned, and to prove how expert we are in our industry, but sometimes we focus too much on industry-specific words. Even if it's not the industry jargon, you want to say things as simply as possible.

Honing the Message

As Servant Warriors, the Triple Bind is one of the kindest phrases we can use with a prospect because we know too much. We could sit with someone for days talking about our product or service, so we need to narrow it down in order to give a sales message most pertinent to that buyer. We don't want to spend much time relaying information the customer doesn't care about yet. We respect the buyer's time. Delivering a sales message is equally about knowing what to edit as what to say. The great thing about the Triple Bind is that it's not only giving your prospect an opportunity to tell you what they want and offering you the path forward but also providing you your selling message.

If an item in your list makes you think, *Everybody might not know this about us, but once they find out they want to do business with us*, put it in the Triple Bind. Even if no one has said, "This is why I'm here," but you know that's what tips them over the edge, put that in!

Your Triple Bind should always evolve. Whatever you use today is not always going to be the best Triple Bind, so don't hold on to it too tightly. The things that are most important to your customers today might not be tomorrow.

You need to be a scientist of your own process and step into an observer position so that every day you can reflect and say, "What are the prospects biting on, and what are they not biting on?"

The best coach for any human being is themselves, so be the coach and producer of yourself and your own sales show. You should constantly upgrade and swap and replace, all while separating your ego and your preferences from the process. Be detached from your art for a moment, and challenge yourself to improve every single day.

Triple Binds are not just for inbound leads; you can use them in outbound prospecting as well. One of our clients is having much success while prospecting via LinkedIn or email. The client sends an introductory message with a Triple Bind like "A few main reasons why people are leaving their current supplier is because of blank, blank, and blank. If any of these three things are a problem that you are currently having or an area that you are wanting to improve, I'd love to have a further conversation." They even use a Triple Bind for setting up a time to talk! They say, "I'd love to have a conversation with you. I'm available at this time, this time, or this time. Of those three, which works best for you? If none do, please offer other suggestions."

One of the objections I hear about the Triple Bind is that it doesn't feel personal enough. I know some sales professionals want to custom-tailor every bit of their conversation. And I get it. Sales professionals have been taught for years that allowing the prospect to guide the conversation is doing what the prospect wants. It's perfectly natural to feel some resistance to the Triple Bind. Based on our own research and polling, prospective buyers are tired of how much work they have to do to buy something, how slow the buying process proceeds, and how much unnecessary small talk they make when they have such little time. With a process, you don't have to guess about what to do in a certain situation. You have clearly defined milestones and goals with every customer in every situation. You do everything you possibly can to move a sale forward. And that's the most powerful outlook you can have as a Sales Warrior. To end the sale strong, you must start strong.

CHAPTER 6

Step 2: The Discovery 360

You learn what the buyer wants and doesn't want. This takes out the guesswork of what I thought they needed and replaces it with their true needs. I now understand what my buyers truly want and need and also what problems they have. It's great to connect on an emotional level here too. It feels good to be able to get customers to trust in you and tell you what their true goals and pain points are.

—Mindy, commercial and military containers

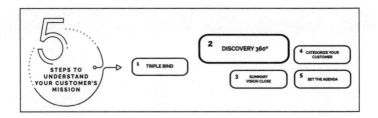

BENEFITS TO THE customer: Gives the opportunity to clarify what customer wants and doesn't want.

Benefits to you: Gives you the map of what information you will need to use in your presentation in order to close the customer.

Let's play a game for a minute: Picture your perfect car. What kind of vehicle is it? What features does it have? How would driving that car benefit you?

What do you like about your current car? What do you not like? What caused you to buy your current car? What aggravates you the most about your current car?

What other cars have you noticed on the road? What have you liked and not liked about the other options you have seen?

From your answers, notice how clear you are on what you want and don't want, what is working for you and what isn't, and what your options are in the market now. It is simple, conversational, and the process for the second step of the Warrior Selling process, the Discovery 360.

The discovery process is simple. Through those questions, I'm trying to discover three main pieces of information: what you want, what you have now, and what else you have seen on the market. As the "prospect," what did you feel as you were answering these questions? Did you feel suddenly curious to explore some of those questions? Did you feel like you were being guided to discover more about your current wants and must-haves? Do you feel like you have discovered more now about your needs than you knew five minutes ago? That's the power of discovery questions, which you'll use to successfully sell to anyone you speak with.

A great way to think of the five steps to understand your customer's mission is to imagine a funnel. You start broad at the top, and you gradually narrow it down so that when you move to the four steps to present a solution, your message will be dialed in and made for the customer. With each step you take, you learn more about your prospect. You ask the tough questions that your competition is too reluctant to ask because you live by the belief that the *why* must be greater than the sacrifice. Their sacrifice could be the cost, time, change, reputation, disruption in their family, friends, company, co-workers, etc. So, you ask these questions to understand their *why* and what is their unique sacrifice if they were to make a change. If you don't get this right, then the rest of the sales process is irrelevant.

In the first step of the five steps to understand your customer's mission, you determined your position of strength by delivering the Triple Bind: "People choose us because of blank, blank, and blank. Of those three, which is a problem you currently need to solve or an area of improvement for you in the future?" Then you presented your unique value proposition over your competitors.

Once you have gained a position of strength, your next goal is to discover the answers to three key things. It doesn't mean you have to word these questions exactly this way, but you need to discover these answers in Step 2.

1 **Want -** *What's your vision for what you want?*
What's important to you about that?

2 **Have -** *What do you like and not like about what you are currently doing?*
What's important to you about that?

3 **Seen -** *What have you liked and not liked about the alternative options that you have seen?*
What's important to you about that?

Here's how a client of mine named Liz used the Discovery 360. Liz was selling to a Fortune 500 company, and the only thing she really knew about it was what she read in the news. She went through the Discovery 360, and she found three vital pieces of information:

- Want: What the prospect really wanted was an advisor to show how to become more profitable. (That opened up some future upsell solutions that the prospect didn't even know the company could do.)

- Have: The company's current supplier had been late on the last few orders, and there had been some invoicing issues.
- Seen: Liz's competition that the prospect had spoken to and researched didn't offer all the services; if Liz wasn't chosen, the Fortune 500 company would have to use two different companies.

How powerful is that? Those are three *huge* pieces of information that Liz discovered to move the sale forward. This information formed the basis for her entire presentation later on. Liz made sure to include in her presentation her company's stats on time from order to delivery. She also shared additional services that she could bundle together to save money and increase profitability, which was the want she got the prospect to verbalize in the first step. She closed that Fortune 500 company, and the Discovery 360 was a vital step that made that happen.

Picture the Discovery 360 as three legs of a tripod. Imagine you use a telescope to find a certain star in the sky. You must have all three of those legs on the telescope strong and stable, or you are off balance. All three are equally important, so find out what the prospect *wants* and how that will benefit the company; the alternatives the prospect has *seen* and are considering, along with what the prospect likes and doesn't like about those alternatives; and what the prospect likes and doesn't like about the current product or service that those in the company *have*. If you miss one of the three, then you're going to miss the star you're looking for. And that star is the next step in the process, the Summary Vision Close, where you summarize exactly what your customer wants, where he or she is coming from, and what the customer likes and doesn't like about options seen so far.

Everybody views the world through the lens of experience, but the only way you can see one's vision is by asking questions about the person's experiences. Your job as a Sales Warrior is to ask great discovery questions so you can do your best to see the world through the customer's eyes, and to understand the customer's perspective—what the prospect is moving away from and moving toward. Once you are there, you can offer solutions that really resonate with the person.

Imagine you are buying your wife a gift, and you tell yourself, *I want to buy my wife this perfect beautiful handbag*. Well, she might see "perfect beautiful handbag" very differently from what you picture. So, you need to know as much from her as possible to make sure that you are in alignment. When you are with your customers, you need to *serve* them by demonstrating what is going to best help *them* and what the best product or service is for *them*.

With the Discovery 360, you are looking not just for things customers don't like but also for what they currently like, what they have, and what they like about their alternatives to you. Knowing what they like has many benefits, all of which will help you close them later. Getting them talking about what they like locks them into that "yes" cadence, which gives you momentum in the sale. All prospects you talk to like *something* about what they currently have; it was what they chose to purchase in the past. Knowing what helped that product win will give you a path to help close your own sale. That's exactly what you need to know so you can remove their fear of leaving the status quo.

Talking about what is working allows prospects to have a full conversation with you, not just one that underscores pain points. It gives them a breather from discussing problems. It also allows them to start collaborating with you, which is important because people naturally want collaboration. They want to feel included. As people communicate, their brains trigger a neurochemical cocktail that makes them feel either good or bad, and we translate that inner experience into words, sentences, and stories. Feel-good conversations trigger higher levels of dopamine, oxytocin, endorphins, and other biochemicals that give us a sense of well-being and safety. That's exactly what you are doing with these questions. It lowers your prospects' guard when you genuinely include them in the process. You are getting around the gatekeeper in their brain. You can remove all that ambiguity, fear, and skepticism by demonstrating that you care about their needs. And that means asking questions.

Some people are nervous about using Discovery 360 to bring up the competition. One client, Jerry, said, "Jason, if I bring up the competition, aren't I just inviting my prospects to think about them?" I told him to write this down and put it on his computer, his steering wheel, and his phone: "Your greatest competition is the conversation you are not present to."

Your prospects don't stop comparing their options once they stop talking with you. They are constantly comparing what you have with your competition. The only way to influence that conversation is to take control of it when your prospect is listening to your presentation. That's what I told Jerry. By diving into the Discovery 360, he took control of conversations.

If your objective is to present a solution to someone, you need to know these three things outlined here. They will help you put your presentation together later.

Always ask what people like and haven't liked about each one, what they want, what they have, and what they have seen. You want to include what they like about what they currently have. Most top Sales Warriors rarely lose sales to the competition, and if they do, that's likely because prospects decided to stay with what they are currently doing. So, if you know what they still like and want, you can include it to reassure them that what they like about the status quo is going to stay, and the things they don't like are all that's changing. People want life improvement but not necessarily change. Without a Sales Warrior, they are in a loop of being unsatisfied, researching solutions, and staying with what they have.

Your job is to stop the loop and send them on a new path. The best way is to start your presentation with everything that would stay the same and then tell them what would be different. This order of the presentation is supported by NLP research, which shows that the majority of people will change if they see the results in that order. Therefore, having knowledge about their current preferences is crucial.

Always remember that your goal with the Discovery 360 isn't to gain ammunition so you can bash the competition. You always want to be respectful of the competition, but you absolutely need to know what you are up against. Think of it like scouting the competition. In professional sports, teams spend hours looking at footage of the competition so they can tailor their own approach to win the game. You always want to give yourself the absolute best chance to close the sale.

The average salesperson will ask questions to figure out what the customers want. The great salesperson will ask questions about what they want *and* what they currently have. The Sales Warrior will ask all those things, along with questions about the competition—and what they like and don't like about the other company.

The best way to overcome any hesitation about competition is to research. Read up on your competition, study it, and have the knowledge to answer your customer's questions about the competition, so you have facts to back up your claims that you are the better option. I tell the teams I coach that if you can't sell for the competition today, you don't know the company well enough. Sales Warriors could sell the competition's products better than salespeople for the company can. Do this exercise. Create a chart that just shows the advantages of your product or service and that of the competitor's, along with both of the disadvantages. This allows you to go into the Discovery 360 armed with the knowledge your customer needs to move forward with you.

A great technique to add to your Discovery 360 is to ask installing questions. For example, let's say you are selling a new home, and you know your prospect has been to another builder's model already, because you asked your Warrior Discovery 360 question, "What other builders have you seen?" Now you can install: "So what were they not able to offer that has you still searching?" You have just installed that the competition couldn't offer everything the customer wanted. Once you get the answer, make a mental note to point that specification out on your home tour.

Here's an example from the business-to-business world. Let's say you are selling IT services and you know your competitor is not fast in handling service tickets. You could lead the prospect: "So what is your expectation for the time a service ticket is resolved?" At that moment, you are installing that the prospect should have an expectation and that the competition probably isn't hitting it.

The eliciting and installation answers give you more personalized information to add to your upcoming pitch, and they also help get the prospect in the right emotional state to be ready to buy.

If your calling is to lead, protect, and serve your customers, then you must know the competition's strengths and weaknesses, along with the customers' wants, needs, expectations, sacrifices, hidden and admitted problems, fears, frustrations, failures, desires, dreams, and destiny. You cannot lead, protect, and serve your prospects as a Sales Warrior unless you know all of it.

A Sales Warrior and a salesperson each have twenty-four hours in the day. Unlike a salesperson, a Sales Warrior knows how to leverage other people's time. If I am on the phone with a prospect and discover that the person has already spoken to one or more sales training companies, I am thrilled because the prospect has already begun to narrow down wants and needs. Now the prospect just has to give me the summary, and I can pick up right where the competition left off. Therefore, you want to talk about the competition early on. It allows you to use your competition's time. Let your competition do 90 percent of the work, but you do the last 10 percent and get paid.

Let's say a customer has already spoken to three salespeople before talking to you, spending at least thirty minutes with each. Before that, the customer spent several hours researching on the internet; talking to coworkers, friends, and family about the problem; and receiving advice. You are leveraging all the hard work that the customer has already done. Instead of annoying the customer by making him or her repeat everything, you start from the summary.

The process will sound like this: "I am glad you were able to speak to XYZ competitor. Tell me, what did you learn from the company that has made you more ready for blank product? Was the salesperson able to discuss with you why this is such a great time to make this kind of purchase? Did the salesperson discuss pricing with you?" You will keep quickly asking questions about the decisions to discover what has already been discussed and is complete, so you know exactly where to pick up the conversation.

You have to remember the positive intention—you are doing this *for* the customer, not *to* the customer. You don't want to waste the customer's time or yours. You are simultaneously being competitive by finding an advantage in the competition's weaknesses. If the competition is not going to achieve resolution or close the customer, that's the competition's fault. I like taking advantage of that situation. It's a noble thing to do—you are serving the customer, leading the person to a place he or she otherwise wouldn't be, and warding off confusion and overcomplication. The worst-case scenario is that your competitors will hate you, but your customers will love you.

Sometimes you are the first person the customer will have called. Maybe your customer says, "Well, you know, you are the first company I've spoken to, but I also have heard of competitor X and want to look at what it has." But you have the knowledge of the competition, so you can say, "Great! Based on what I learn from you today, I'll make a list of how we are the same and how we are different." When you have all this information, you can prevent your prospect from having to go spend time somewhere else and then come back to you.

People have different buying mentalities. For some, as soon as they see something they like, they buy it. They are done buyers; their ultimate goal is to be done, so as soon as something is good enough, they buy it. The other category is the perfect buyer; such buyers have rules like needing to see three options before buying. By talking about the competition, you can give those buyers the experience of seeing other options without leaving you.

Sales Warriors have the courage to pull off taking control of the competitor's conversation. That requires high self-esteem and efficacy in your product or service. You share advantages of your product and perceived advantages of the competitor's. I use language like this: "The people who choose us value a high level of customer experience right from the beginning with their sales team, so they only want the best representing their company. The people who choose competitor X value a lower price and are okay with a new sales recruit not making sales for the first six months. So, Mr. Customer, which one do you value more?" In this scenario, I speak of the benefit of each and explain that both are valid choices that many pick.

The purpose of the Discovery 360 is to find out what they are looking for, what they truly want, what they are trying to accomplish, and why they are trying to accomplish it. You want to find out what they currently have, what they like and don't like about it, and how their life has changed. Ask about how situations change. How had the prospects' life changed so that what they have had no longer fits? How has their business changed, so that product or service no longer works for them? How has their product or service not evolved or adapted with them throughout this change? If you are a Sales Warrior, you'll be able to use that information to hold the position of power by comparing your product favorably to the competition.

Remember, the better questions you ask, the better answers you get, and the easier the rest of the downstream sales process will be for you and your prospects. Lower the importance you place on yourself to close the sale. With the pressure down, you will be able to ask better questions and listen more attentively which will, ironically, lead to more sales.

CHAPTER 7

Step 3: The Summary Vision Close

This step paints the picture of what the prospect's new future will look like with your solution in mind as the answer. . . . Without the Summary Vision Close, sales professionals will often move too quickly to the close without painting the picture of what the resolution will actually look like.

—Paul, business franchising

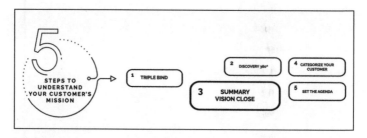

BENEFITS TO THE customer: Gives certainty that you understand customer's vision for the ideal solution.

Benefits to you: Helps you gain rapport and continue to move the sale forward.

In this chapter, you are going to learn how to get on the same page with your prospects by using the Summary Vision Close. In this step, you'll gain rapport and continue to move the sale forward.

You have probably heard a lot of different definitions for *rapport* in your sales career. You may have heard that it means creating a friendship, making small talk to break the ice, or talking about the prospects' awards on the walls of their office (or their LinkedIn profile). But it's so important for your impact as a Sales Warrior to understand what true rapport means. Rapport in a selling situation means you are on the same page with your prospects and gaining agreement that you both see the problem and desired outcome the same way.

I remember listening to a sales trainer define *rapport* as "getting the prospect to like you and to be your friend." He taught that rapport is important because people buy from people they like. The problem with locking in to this belief is that getting people to like you isn't real rapport, and honestly, it just isn't that important. I like many people whom I haven't purchased from. Just the same, I've purchased from people I respect but don't necessarily like.

Real sales rapport means sharing a mutual purpose and mutual respect. What it does *not* mean is being liked. Your goal is not to get this person to invite you over for Thanksgiving dinner. When your positive intention is to be *liked*, and not to get on the same page, you are derailing your own sale by asking dead-end questions, which waste time and lead to indecision from your buyer. One thing we know about the human brain is that uncertainty and indecision wreak havoc on our decision-making ability. To survive, the human brain evolved to be uncertainty averse. When things become less predictable and less controllable, people are threatened. Uncertainty also leads to decreases in motivation, focus, agility, cooperative behavior, self-control, a sense of purpose and meaning, and overall well-being. Dealing with indecision isn't something people have evolved to do very well. In other words, uncertainty stops sales.

Remember, the Sales Warrior gives certainty plus education *with* rapport. The one constant all along the way is that baseline of rapport. Your goal is to gain it and then keep it throughout the sale. That's how you know you are improving customers' lives and moving a sale forward.

The best way to determine if you have rapport is by using the Summary Vision Close. Once you have established your position of strength and asked your discovery questions, it's time to make sure you understand customers' goals by echoing back what they already told you.

This is how to structure your Summary Vision Close:

> *"So you said you're looking for _____ because of ____, and you want to get away from ____ so you can _____* **does that sound like what you're looking for?"**

You want to make sure you use what customers are moving toward and what they are moving away from. If they are moving *toward* a faster production cycle, then they are moving *away* from revenue loss and missed deadlines. They may move *toward* a bigger home and *away* from a cramped living space. They move *toward* an environmentally friendly option and *away* from waste and pollution. You want to express both sides of it, so you are connecting with them regardless of whether they are a move-toward person or a move-away person.

Using both language patterns is crucial because they are one of the major meta patterns in the brain. For instance, think of the last time you decided to purchase a car. What brought you to that decision? Either the new model just came out and is better than last year's model, and you really want to have it, or your old car is falling apart and is no longer safe to drive. Feel the difference? One type of person buys by moving toward the new, and the other type buys to move away from the old. When you work with someone new, you might not know which way the person leans. And also, more often than not, you are selling to more than one person at a time. Your safest bet is to speak in both. To make it easy, I scripted it out with blanks for you to fill in both. That way, you don't err by only speaking in the way your brain is wired.

"So, you said you were looking for _____ (move toward) because of _____, and that you want to get away from _____ (move away) so you can _____. Does that sound like what you are looking for?"

The language aligns with the philosophy of selling at the very beginning of the book: all human beings move away from pain and toward life improvement, and the Sales Warrior's mission is to liberate them from any indecision. Describing both perspectives positions you as the advisor for the rest of the sale.

If my Triple Bind revealed that my position of strength was my program-based training versus event-based training for each client, and my Discovery 360 revealed the prospect was struggling to meet a high sales goal, utilizing a current training solution of watching self-guided videos that the sales team was not applying, and considering an alternative that doesn't teach mindset, then my Summary Vision Close would be like this: "You said you are looking for highly accountable training that gets more salespeople up to speed faster because you have a huge sales goal to hit this year. And you want to get away from self-guided training because it isn't helping you achieve that goal, and you are also considering XYZ training but are concerned that it won't stick because it doesn't teach mindset. Does that sound like what you are looking for?"

Down the road, I can connect my VETO Selling Message (Step 6) to their lack of results with their current training as well as the competition's pitfall of not teaching the mindset along with the process. People don't argue with their own advice. All you are doing is confirming things the prospect already said so you can lead that person to the next step.

One of the beliefs of Warrior Selling is that the purpose of selling is to convince the "just looking" prospect to buy from you today over all alternatives. You want to know what they like and don't like so you can position your value over what they currently have. You gained that information with the Discovery 360, and now you are getting on the same page with the Summary Vision Close. Having rapport is crucial to achieving resolution, and the Summary Vision Close is the best way to do it. By knowing what is most important to the prospect, you can tailor your message to what is most relevant to move the sale forward. Just those small tweaks in your language pattern make all the difference.

The most common objection I hear from salespeople around the Summary Vision Close is: "I sell by making relationships. That's what rapport means to me."

Relationships with your prospects are a great thing. The problem is in how one defines *relationship* and, more specifically, the passive behaviors that implies. A Sales Warrior's primary question is "How can I move a sale forward today?" It's not "How can I develop a relationship today?" The great news is that you probably already believe this; you just need to change the way you look at things.

A successful client of mine named Gina had a similar objection. She confided that she didn't want to change her sales approach because it was working and because she loved the relationships she had with her clients. She was concerned that I was going to make her end those friendships and stress that she only talk business with them. I understood why she was concerned and let her know that I, too, had strong friendships with many of my clients that I would not want to end. When I asked her to take me through her process, I understood she was confusing the terms *friendly* and *friendship*. She had a great process, but her leash was that she couldn't be assertive and friendly at the same time. That's not the case—it's great to be friendly so long as you realize that your goal is total and complete resolution, not to make a friend. She was a top 1 percent Sales Warrior because she took the lead. She just had to change the way she looked at things, so the things she looked at changed.

We are all human—we make mistakes, and sometimes we just miss things. That has nothing to do with skill or experience. Mistakes can even happen with your close friends or family. Sometimes we misunderstand our closest friends, so it is even more important that we ensure we correctly understand our prospects and our customers, even if we have worked with them for years.

The customers are unable to hear what you have to offer them until they feel understood in their situation and problem. When they feel like they have been heard, and you are both on the same page, only then can you move forward together. We all desire to express ourselves and to be understood. Your customers will experience a subconscious relief that you are serving them instead of talking over them and not paying attention to what they have shared. Using the Summary Vision Close allows them to have more faith in you and have more courage to express more to you. The more you demonstrate that you understand, the more willing they will be to express more, share more detail, and give you more feedback.

Have you ever had someone just stop talking during a conversation? More often than not, it's not about something that *happened* but instead about what *didn't happen*. The Summary Vision Close was missing, and the person did not feel understood or listened to. You didn't understand the person's needs, so now the prospect doesn't feel like sharing anymore!

Anytime we see somebody start to shut down or start to get quiet, it's because the customer feels we are not giving them presence and listening to them. Hence, their internal self-talk said, "What is the point of sharing this information with the sales professional? I will just figure this out myself."

We missed something along the way, and they no longer feel heard and understood.

My belief system is that I believe people really do want to be sold, and they want to buy! They want to be convinced that this is the best use of their time and money, and they want to feel wanted and important, but not by being manipulated or conned. Manipulation is trying to convince someone to do something when it only benefits you. Persuasion is convincing someone to do something in the person's best interest. That allows the customer to surrender and ease into the process, knowing you are both on the journey, working together as a team to make success happen. I know I want that when I spend my money; I love going through those experiences!

Summary Vision Close is an easy step to execute, but sometimes it is easier not to. Salespeople make a huge mistake when they don't summarize exactly what the customer has shared with them and skip to the Summary Vision Close. What pain are they moving away from? What is the life improvement the customer wants to move toward?

CHAPTER 8

Step 4: Categorize Your Buyer

One of my favorite steps and probably the most important [is categorizing your buyer]. Everything after this point is based on what category they are. Prior to learning this step, I experienced misalignment with the client, and [categorizing the buyer] allowed me to understand where the buyer currently is.

—Trenton, homebuilding

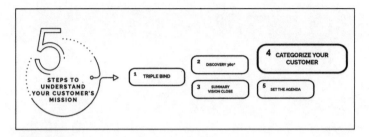

BENEFITS TO THE customer: Builds rapport because you are working with buyer wherever they buyer is in the buying process.

Benefits to you: Stops you from wasting your energy giving the wrong selling message to the prospect.

What the Categories Are Not

Before I can teach you how to categorize your buyer, I must first teach you what the categories are and what they are not. They are not the old-school A, B, and C prospects. ABC is dead!

You have probably been taught to have strong elevator pitches and go into the conversation talking about your product, your company, your mission, and your story. Sales professionals have been mistakenly taught to give their company story in the first five minutes, but based on our research, that strategy only works for prospects at the end of their journey and about to make the decision as to which company to move forward with. In the Warrior Selling process, this is a Category 3 buyer, which accounts for less than 15 percent and closer to 2 percent of your first-encounter prospect conversations.

You need to organize your sales process and see it as a method. Identify the category, know what the prospect's problem is, execute the appropriate strategy and selling messages, and chunk it down to the appropriate decisions that keep the prospect from moving forward to the next category. This takes the guesswork out of your prospect and pipeline and improves your sales forecast accuracy.

Most salespeople are familiar with the ABC rating model, which is the ready, willing, and able system, normally used to distinguish between their prospects based on when the prospect wants to buy. The A prospects say they want to buy soon, B prospects say they are going to buy somewhere in the near future, and C prospects seemingly will take the longest time to buy. Some companies try to put time frames on the categories, but even then, they are very subjective. The problem with the ABC method is it puts all the energy and position of strength on whether the *customer* comes in ready, willing, and able to buy.

When salespeople who use the ABC method of categorizing buyers were surveyed on how they knew someone was an A prospect and ready, willing, and able to purchase, here is what they said:

- "I know they are ready and willing because they have been agreeable to my presentation."
- "They talk about how much they are interested in our services."
- "They are willing because they are asking me a lot of questions."

- "I know they are willing because they haven't had a lot of overall concerns."
- "[I know] because I've spoken to multiple decision-makers. I've had five conversations with them in thirty days."

The method is scary and unfair to the salespeople because their income is dependent on moving people forward in the sales process. Their livelihood is riding on these subjective rules they have created around ABC prospects. I get charged up about this because sales trainers accept money to teach something that is not setting salespeople up for success.

Now, the Sales Warriors believe that it's their job to *make* their prospects ready, willing, and sometimes even able to buy. So, the ABC method does not apply. The categories I am about to teach you are better and more objective methods to focus on. It's a progression in the sale. I have a number one, who are "just looking," a number two, who are "overwhelmed," and a number three, who are "torn." If you stay focused on resolving the decisions that resolve the individual category, then you'll be in control of the sale no matter the circumstances.

What the Categories Are

Every single prospect is in one of three categories:

- Category 1: The "just looking" buyer. This buyer has not decided to make a change to the status quo.

- Category 2: The overwhelmed buyer. This buyer has decided to make a change but is overwhelmed by all the options.
- Category 3: The torn buyer. This buyer is torn between you and a competitor.

If you are not categorizing your buyers properly, you give the wrong selling message to the buyer in front of you. Almost all sales professionals I speak to have a solid and well-polished sales message on why to purchase them over the competition. However, that sales message is only good for the Category 3 buyers. Depending on the market, our research shows that only 2 to 15 percent of buyers rate as Category 3. That means 85 to 98 percent of your prospects are not ready to hear that sales message. Depressing, right? You can feel sharp, look fresh, work your tail off, and give the performance of your life, and it won't matter because prospects can't hear it.

The right selling message with the wrong buyer is the same as the wrong selling message with the right buyer. You must create sales messages that are just as strong for both your Category 1 buyers and your Category 2 buyers. Your message for your Category 1 buyer is "Why leave what you have?" You cannot convince that person to buy from you until you have convinced the buyer to stop the status quo.

Your purpose with Category 1 buyers is to get them to burn the boats. This concept comes from sixteenth-century Spanish conquistador Hernán Cortés, who led an expedition into Mexico that resulted in the fall of the Aztec empire. It is said that when their boats arrived on the Mexican coast, he looked at his commanders and said, "Burn the boats." It was now understood by his troops that they were to conquer Mexico or die trying; there was no turning around and going back to their previous life. Cortes wanted to ensure his troops were committed to moving forward. He knew he couldn't win unless he removed the option of retreat.

I love this metaphor because it cements this step. Did you get the customer to burn the boats? Is he or she committed only to moving forward? Has the customer decided that, regardless of whether they buy from you, there is no option to go back to their previous life? The option of going back to the home, vendor, manufacturer, car, software solution, and so forth must be off the table. It's a clear yes or no. If you are not sure, then it is a no. If yes, prove it. What specifically did you ask, and what response determined that? Was it a committed burn the boat? Or was it a maybe or probably? Those answers are lifeboats back to the previous life.

The selling messages that you must master in this category are "Why leave what you have?" and "Why buy now?" Unless you ask, you don't know. We lose sales to not only the competition but also, and mostly, to people not making a change. Most people stay with the familiar comfortable solution versus the solution perceived as better but still unknown. Where has most of your previous sales training been focused? Is it how to sell against the competitor, why buy your specific product or service, or why buy from your company brand? But because you lose most of your sales to people *not making* a change, you must first convince them they need to change; the time today to make the change is worth the perceived risk, and the sooner they act, the sooner their life, their family, their department, or their company's life will improve. You must accomplish this *before* you convince them of anything else, or you are wasting both of your time.

The hardest sale to make is convincing your prospect to make a change. In our own research, polling thousands of sales professionals around the world, we found that depending on the market, 50 to 70 percent of all prospects enter the sales relationship as a Category 1 buyer. Less than 20 percent of those Category 1 buyers will have a second conversation with a sales professional. If you have ten Category 1 buyers, you are only going to end up talking to two of them a second time. That's not on the buyer—that's because you're not using the right selling message with them. If you use the correct selling message with a Category 1 buyer, then you will end up spending more time with your prospect, and your percentage of second conversations will increase.

I cannot convince someone to purchase recruiting services or training from me until I convince the person that having the sales manager recruit takes too much time away from the sales team and is costing more money than realized. That's the same with training services—I cannot sell FPG for sales training if the customer is not convinced that the team should be trained or thinks the current book study is enough.

Customers can't really hear all the brilliance of your sales message on your CRM system if they are not convinced that their current system isn't working. They can't buy a new home until they decide to move from their current home. And they can't choose the Jaguar you are selling over the Mercedes until they first decide they don't want their Range Rover. Remember, more sales are lost to the prospect staying with the status quo than to a different competitor. This makes the Category 1 message arguably the most important selling message you have.

The Category 2 buyer is overwhelmed after making the hardest decision, which led to the need for even more decisions: pricing, timing, types of solutions, locations, and the like. If your purpose for Category 1 is to get buyers to burn the boats and make a change, then the purpose for a Category 2 buyers is to narrow their options to no more than three. You do this by creating a hierarchy of criteria for them. The prospects can't get everything they want based on their timing, budget, location needs, customization, and the rest. You must lead them to determine what their needs, wants, and expectations are, and, lastly, what they are willing to sacrifice. After the options are narrowed, they can become Category 3 buyers.

The Category 2 message is "Why buy the genre of product you are selling?" In my world, the problem someone shows up with is the need for more sales.

What I am selling is more Sales Warriors for the team, either from a recruiting perspective or by training up the current sales professionals. My solutions are not the only ones, even though they are the best. Sometimes people consider a new CRM system, thinking that if they had more data or reports, the salesperson could see how to get more sales. Sometimes they also consider hiring a new marketing company, thinking that more leads, even with their 2 percent conversion rate, can change the number of sales. With Category 2 buyers, my sales message must convince them to move forward with recruiting and training. I must get them to decide that CRM systems and websites are no longer options.

Let's look at this from the new home perspective. A buyer deciding to leave the current home doesn't necessitate a new home from a builder. The buyer still has options: buying resale, renting, and moving into the parent's basement. Okay, the basement probably wouldn't work, but realize the buyer isn't ready to say yes to you yet. First, you must convincingly present a new home over a resale and over renting. Only then would you move on to your Category 3 message.

Your selling message for the Category 3 customer, the torn buyer, is "Why buy here?" You have probably already created, polished, and perfected the message. If so, make sure it fits all of the criteria and plug it in. If you don't have this message created yet, don't worry; I will show you a structure to create it now.

In a perfect world your prospect is torn between three of *your* options, but in most scenarios, the prospect is torn between you and a competitor. Your purpose here is to lead the person to resolution. If you do, you'll win. If you apply pressure to choose you, you will create resistance, which will cause uncertainty. I am not saying be a soft closer; I am saying be an assertive hard closer but toward the solution best for the prospect.

Sometimes the prospect decides that the competitor is best at that time, but at least it happens *on your terms* and not behind your back. At least you still sold the prospect on deciding to improve his or her life; your competition didn't do so. Your competition just got a market sale from your Warrior process. Don't worry about losing this one, because *if you commit to closing every prospect to decide either with you or your competition, then you officially have a 100 percent conversion rate.* And even though you lost that one sale, you will win more than anyone else.

If you want to make market-based, circumstantial money, only focus on converting Category 2 and 3 buyers, the ones everyone else is going after. All your competitors are going after the smallest pool of buyers. The overwhelming majority of buyers, typically around 50 percent of them, are those of Category 1; they haven't decided to make a change. You can be the one Sales Warrior who goes after the buyers your competitors are too afraid to sell. I promise you that when you focus on Category 1, true just-looking buyers, you will not only stand out from everyone else but also have the highest customer satisfaction. When you convince the Category 1 buyer to change, that buyer will trust you all along the way, which will lead to more income for you and more market share for your company.

This is true because you have been through it all together. The penultimate Warrior Selling belief is "A Warrior sale must involve conflict, compromise, and collaboration and challenge perspective." You will make many Warrior sales after someone starts with you at the beginning of the journey. Our research has shown a higher percentage of referrals, and more referrals from a customer, among those who started their journey with the Sales Warrior under Category 1 versus under Category 2 or 3.

I created this system that would allow the Sales Warrior to be objective about where the customer is in the process and to give a tactical process to follow based on what was discovered. Within each of the categories are decisions the prospect needs to make. For instance, to complete Category 1, the prospect must decide two things: that the current solution is unsatisfactory and that a change is financially possible. There are more decisions, but this gives you an idea. If you start with Category 1 and resolve all the Category 1 decisions and selling messages, then you can move on to Category 2. It's like levels in a game.

I transitioned Andrew, a financial advisor, from the ABC method to the three categories. Andrew was working with what he had decided was an A prospect.

He thought he had a hot one, a big sale. I asked him the following:

- "Does she agree that your services are better than everyone else's?" He said no.
- "Is she willing to miss out on what she wants?" He wasn't sure.
- "Is she going to choose you over all alternatives?" He wasn't sure.
- "Is she excited and proud of your brand?" He wasn't sure.
- "Has she bought into you as her advisor, and is she learning things she didn't already know?" He thought so.
- "Does she believe that your service is the best possible choice?" He wasn't sure.
- "Is she unsatisfied with her current service?" He wasn't sure.
- "Is she secure in the economy?" He said no.
- "Is she sure she can afford it?" He said no.
- "Does she have a budget?" He wasn't sure.
- "Does she want to spend the money?" He wasn't sure.

Based on those questions, Andrew realized he wasn't on the verge of closing. In fact, he barely had what I classify as Category 1!

Andrew isn't alone. His prospect's willingness to hear from him and her compliance and interest on the phone does not translate into a sale. What Andrew saw as an A (analogous to Category 3) was just barely Category 1. This ABC subjective rating system, taught for decades, is ingrained in every CRM out there. It needs to be stopped because it wastes the time and hurts the livelihood of commission-based salespeople. Once Andrew was able to see that his prospect was in Category 1, he changed his selling message to "Why leave what you have?" and started to truly move the prospect forward. Previously, he had spoken to the prospect five times; after this reframing, she was closed with only two more conversations.

HubSpot reports that sales turnover is nearly three times higher than any other industry.[4] Sirius Decisions data also shows that almost half (45 percent) of B2B sales organizations have turnover rates above 30 percent.[5]

One of my beliefs about why salespeople fail is that they don't know how to win, and the ABC method is a major part of the problem. Not knowing how to win creates a tremendous amount of stress and self-doubt. And when salespeople aren't winning and there's no disciplined forecasting strategy based on objective reality, companies make reckless decisions on hiring employees and investing in new systems, all based on poor forecasting and an outdated subjective system of ABC.

The cure is organizing your prospects based on the three categories, which will help the salesperson know what message to give the prospect and help the sales manager properly forecast sales. And a good sales forecast helps the CEO and COO make smart financial and hiring decisions and keep the company profitable.

I want to show you how to win. I want to give you the rules of the game so your forecast and your income are no longer up to chance—and you can predict them accurately.

Each week in sales offices across the nation, sales managers ask their teams, "How many sales are you going to make this week?" Salespeople must come up with a number. When this happens to you, what goes through your mind? Maybe you think something like this: *I've talked to Prospect Y five times in the past week. I'll bet he is going to buy. And Prospect Z I've talked to eight times this month, and she seems really interested—this has got to be the week that she is ready to buy."*

What is wrong with that strategy? Maybe you are not the only option those buyers have talked to. Maybe the reason they haven't decided is that they don't know if they have found the right option yet. Maybe they are dragging their feet because they are scared about the economy.

Here's what else you could think: *I need to say zero, but I am not allowed to say that. So I'll play it safe and say one.*

Do you remember the good news I gave you at the beginning of this book? You don't have to fumble for an answer—you can know it. When you follow the process of creating emotional urgency, you can look at the list of selling messages and pinpoint where each customer stands. When your manager asks you how many sales you are going to make, you can have a real answer ready.

People are buying in today's market. The only question is, whom are they buying from? They are buying from the Sales Warriors who separate themselves from the rest by believing, thinking, feeling, acting, and executing their sales process differently.

If you think not selling your prospect on you or your company until you two arrive at Category 3 doesn't seem right, that is a leash. Normally, you may want to sell someone on your business, story, and values right away, but research has shown that the customers don't care about your company or you until they are torn between you and your competition. Until then, the sales process is about them and not about you. When customers are in Category 1, they are just deciding if their *why* is greater than the sacrifice. If you are familiar with selling software as a service (SAAS) or have been on the buying side of new software for your company, you understand this concept. You know that customers must be convinced that what they are currently doing is not working before they can be willing to hear your unique solution. Changing their current software requires a lot of work, and your customers need to want that change before they are willing to learn about your unique company and values.

When I was creating the Warrior Selling 5/4/3 Factor, before it even had the name, it was only a handful of steps, and categorizing prospects was one of them.

That's how crucial this is. The entire process in this book evolved from this step.

Categorizing prospects came from the desire to remove the guesswork from income. Salespeople have always struggled to estimate weekly sales for the sales manager. It was always a guessing game, as if salespeople are psychics. The answers ranged from, "I've got a hot one," to "I feel good about this one," to "I can just tell." Salespeople are being asked how many sales they are going to get without a standard way to identify them. So, they are in essence being asked to look deep into the eyes of the prospect and feel whether or not that person is going to buy. It's as if we are asking them to be psychics, mind readers, or as I call them, "sales whisperers."

Now, when my salespeople come off of a sales call, I just ask them, "What was the category of the buyer?" Now, at the beginning of every week, I ask my salespeople, "How many Category 1s do you have? How many 2s or 3s?" This is *the* step. If you remember one step from this book, this would be the one, because the whole process evolves from here.

The following graphics clearly show your strategy with each category of buyer. You need to use an appropriate selling message to convince a Category 1 prospect to move to Category 2, from Category 2 to Category 3, and from Category 3 to closed. If you don't match the right strategy with the appropriate category of buyer, you'll fail to convert the sale.

Step 4: Categorize Your Buyer

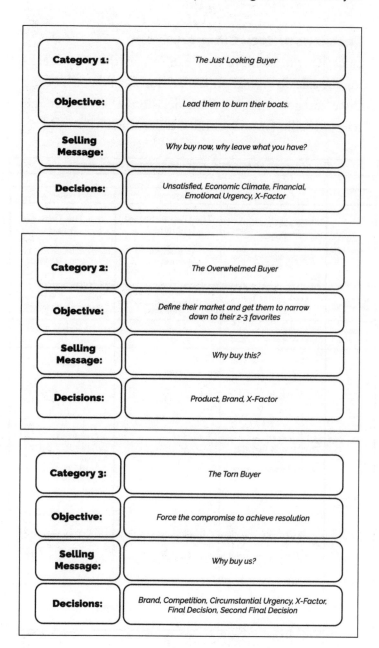

Category 1:	The Just Looking Buyer
Objective:	Lead them to burn their boats.
Selling Message:	Why buy now, why leave what you have?
Decisions:	Unsatisfied, Economic Climate, Financial, Emotional Urgency, X-Factor

Category 2:	The Overwhelmed Buyer
Objective:	Define their market and get them to narrow down to their 2-3 favorites
Selling Message:	Why buy this?
Decisions:	Product, Brand, X-Factor

Category 3:	The Torn Buyer
Objective:	Force the compromise to achieve resolution
Selling Message:	Why buy us?
Decisions:	Brand, Competition, Circumstantial Urgency, X-Factor, Final Decision, Second Final Decision

Decisions of Each Category

Sales Warriors believe they can sell anything by breaking the sale down into small decisions. Inside each of the three categories are relevant decisions that answer the relevant selling message and advance the sale forward.

THE 4 STEPS TO EFFICIENT & EFFECTIVE SELLING "CHEAT SHEET"		
	CATEGORY 1	**CATEGORY 2**	**CATEGORY 3**

	CATEGORY 1	**CATEGORY 2**	**CATEGORY 3**
STEP 1: DETERMINE	**The Just Looking Buyer** Has not decided to do something.	**The Overwhelmed Buyer** Has decided to do something, but doesn't know what.	**The Torn Buyer** Has decided to do something but is torn between 2-3 options.
STEP 2: OBJECTIVE	Lead them to "burn their boats."	Define their market and get them to narrow down to their 2-3 favorites.	Force the compromise to achieve resolution.
STEP 3: MESSAGE	"Why buy now..." "Why leave what you have..."	"Why buy this..."	"Why buy us..."
STEP 4: DECISIONS	1. Unsatisfied 2. Economic Climate 3. Financial 4. Emotional Urgency	1. Product	1. Competition 2. Circumstancial Urgency 3. Final Decision 4. Second Final Decision
		Brand	
	X- Factor		

For a Category 1 buyer, the relevant decisions fall under these classifications:

- Unsatisfied
- Economic Climate
- Financial
- Emotional Urgency
- X-Factor

For a Category 2 buyer, the relevant decisions have these classifications:

- Product
- Brand
- X-Factor

For a Category 3 buyer, the relevant decisions fall under these classifications:

- Brand
- Competition
- Circumstantial Urgency
- X-Factor
- Final Decision
- Second Final Decision

Make sure you can answer each of the following questions for your prospects. The only reason the sale will ever pause and you will lose a sale is when you can't answer the following questions:

- **Unsatisfied**: What would customers like to change with their current product or service? How has their life and or business changed as a result of the current product or service failing them? What pain is their current product or service causing?
- **Economic Climate**: How do customers feel about the current economic impacts of their decision to make a change? Do they feel safe making a change in the current economy?
- **Financial**: Is this purchase within their affordability? Do they understand and feel confident about the total cost of ownership? Do they feel confident about the return on investment?
- **Emotional Urgency**: What would improve in their personal or business life if they were to move forward with this product or service today? If they don't solve their current problem, then what will that mean to them?
- **X-Factor**: How has their experience been with other sales professionals? What are you doing to stand out? What did you do to show them you are their protector, leader, and servant in this purchase?

- **Product:** How does your product or service improve their life? What does it do for them that their current product doesn't? How is it better than their current product or service?
- **Brand:** Do customers identify with your brand? Does your brand have values similar to what they are looking for? Do they understand your brand promise, and are they in alignment with your unique way of doing business?
- **Competition:** Who is the alternative if they don't buy from us? What advantages does the competition have over us? What advantages do we have over the competition? What is the price difference between you and your competitor? If your product or service is more expensive, how are you proving your value?
- **Circumstantial Urgency:** What timing needs do customers have? How can you leverage your current inventory, time of year, and price increases to create the feeling of missing out?
- **Final Decision:** Did you present three great options? Did you lead customers to eliminate an option, and did you assumptive-close the final option?
- **Second Final Decision:** Did you upsell them? Did you uncover who the alternative is if they don't move forward with you? What were the objections, and how did you handle them?

Did you close again? Did you give them an assignment? Did you schedule a follow-up meeting with them?

Notice that some of these decisions span more than one category. That is because they can be answered at any time and are decisions you need to keep emphasizing as the sale moves forward.

The order of the decisions is important as well. Imagine you are on a blind date, and this person, whom you have just met for the first time, says, "Let me tell you about my family. They came here hundreds of years ago from Italy, and my grandfather went through this experience as a child, and then he grew up and married this woman and had my mom's half-sister, and then they got divorced, and he met my grandmother, and let me tell you about my mother, she did this and that!"

How odd would that be? You are there to get to know that person, but you want to get to know *that person*, to see if the current individual is compatible with the current you. Once the relationship progresses, then you are more apt to want to know about family and history. *Later* in the relationship, you want to know everything! But when you first meet each other, that is a lot of intense information to start with.

It's the same with your customers. If you are jumping right into "let me tell you the history of our company," it's frustrating to the prospect. If you don't categorize them and jump right into the Category 3 decisions and messaging, it's exactly like sitting down on the first date and saying, "Here's why you should move forward with marrying me." You have to build rapport, get on the same page, and see where you are and where you are going.

How to Categorize

Up to this point, you have been gathering information, establishing the position of strength, and developing rapport so you can set up your selling message. To *determine* that selling message, ask, "So, based on what we've discussed, have you definitely decided to leave what you have?"

If the answer is no, then you know you have a true Category 1, just-looking buyer on your hands. The buyer hasn't decided to move forward with any options and doesn't see enough value around what you offer. If that's the case, you'll just move forward to the fifth step to set the agenda for your presentation. If the buyer said yes, then to determine whether the buyer fits Category 2 or 3 ask, "Have you definitely decided to move forward with _____?" (The blank would be a type of company.)

For example, in my world, the question would be something like "Have you definitely decided to move forward with a program-based training company?" Or, "Have you definitely decided to move forward with a full-service, sales-specific recruiting company?"

Following the earlier examples of new homes and CRM systems, it would be "Have you definitely decided to move forward with building a new home?" Or, "Have you definitely decided to move forward with purchasing a CRM system for your company?"

If the prospect answers yes, then you will know they fit in Category 3, the torn buyers, and you can proceed with that sales message and resolve Category 3 decisions. If the answer is no, then you will know the buyer fits in Category 2, and you can proceed with those decisions and selling message.

Here is why this is so important: The *vast* majority of your initial prospects are true Category 1, just-looking buyers. That doesn't mean you'll *never* see a customer who has decided to buy already, but most customers haven't. Regarding B2B sales, a recent Google study found that, on average, just 7 percent of any B2B company is actively buying something at any given time—7 percent. That means you have 93 percent of the market at any given time just waiting for you to convince them and to fix the problems they already know about and even fix the problems they don't know they have. A Sales Warrior gets motivated by that. A Sales Warrior believes that you get just-looking buyers to buy faster than they intended and for more money than they planned because the sooner they act, the sooner their life will improve.

The biggest pitfall sales professionals fall into with this step is to get too creative with it. With this step, it is best to always just stick to the exact script. This is an area where you want to make sure communication is clear, so using direct language is best.

Just say, "Does that mean that you are *definitely* making a change? Does that mean that you are *definitely* leaving what you have? Does that mean that you are *definitely* moving forward with another machine provider?"

And please, for you, don't remove the word definitely. If you ask the buyer, "Have you decided to make a change?" The customer could answer yes and feel more than 50 likely. But if you ask if that customer has definitely decided to make a change, it disrupts the normal brain patterns, and the buyer is more likely to answer yes only if 100 percent sure.

I know some people reading this struggle with following an exact script every single time, but you will have the best results when you do. I follow this exact script every single time, and I'd never remove *definitely* from the question.

Almost all prospects come to us using Category 3 language. Your job as a Sales Warrior is to not fall into the excitement trap of agreeing with their language patterns until you have verified their category through the questions.

I was working with a Sales Warrior named Tyler who sells commercial design and furniture and was very excited because a prospect had just let him know a final decision on which company would be outfitting the new building was forthcoming. The decision was between Tyler and one other company, and so Tyler gave his Category 3 sales message beautifully and felt very confident that he would be getting a signed contract the next day. But the next day came and went with no communication. Tyler started reaching out, first by phone, then email, then text—crickets. Tyler had been ghosted.

Weeks later, he was able to get his prospect back on the phone. He needed to know what had happened. The prospect apologized for not getting back in touch sooner but let Tyler know the company decided to use the money elsewhere and instead of buying new office furniture would just reuse the furniture from the current office. Buyers many times speak Category 3 language without removing what they are currently doing. Tyler learned this the hard way. He told me that he will never skip categorizing his buyers again.

Categorizing your buyers removes that guesswork and risk by objectively looking at where your buyers are in the sales process. If the buyer has said, "I'm *definitely* making change," that alters your entire selling message! Now you can say, "Since you are definitely making a change, now let us narrow down your options to determine what is most important to you. If we don't, you can get overwhelmed real quickly," or, if the buyer is in Category 3, "Now that you are clear on exactly what is most important to you, let us decide what is the overall best option that you should move forward with today."

So often, we think we've closed the buyer on the category or on one of the decisions because of some story we tell ourselves. Maybe we feel like we've convinced the buyer on our product or service, or our customer service, or our brand, but we never got verbal confirmation of our solution. Why is this so important? When you get to the next stage of the sale, the three steps to resolve the sale and close the customer, the decisions that will stop your sale cold are the ones you didn't mutually agree upon. So, all along the way, make sure you get the customer to verbalize their agreement so that you have no loose ends.

CHAPTER 9

Step 5:
Set the Agenda

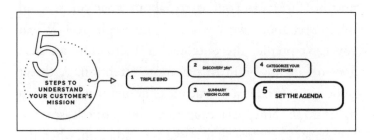

This helps you keep on track, gets you a good idea of what the meeting will look like, helps you meet your goals, gives you the position of strength, helps you stay organized, helps you be more efficient, helps you get to the beach, and [helps] make sure you are not missing something. You are

making sure that they have a clear idea of what the appointment is going to look like and help build rapport on what to expect in the next steps.
—Cory, general contractor

BENEFITS TO THE customer: Gives customer certainty and confidence in the next steps.

Benefits to you: Gives you the path to move the sale forward.

Now that you have accomplished the four steps, it's time to set the agenda for how you are going to present your solutions that solve the customer's problems. This step is about certainty and letting your prospect know what is coming next as you present your solutions.

Your brain loves certainty because it helps you stay alive. Your brain is constantly making predictions about possible threats to your safety, about what you see and might see, about what you feel and might feel. When you can't predict the outcome of a situation, an alert goes off in the brain to pay more attention. A threat response occurs. Just a little bit of ambiguity on its own lights up the amygdala, causing the body to release stress hormones like cortisol. Just like any addiction, when the craving for certainty is met, the release of dopamine gives a sensation of reward.

For us, that means putting our prospects in the buyer's state; we need to help them release dopamine. The brain connects uncertainty with pain, and the philosophy of a Sales Warrior is that all human beings move away from pain and toward life improvement. A Sales Warrior's mission is to liberate them from any indecision. Your prospects are *biologically* trying to avoid uncertainty. To avoid that pain and release that reward chemical, they need certainty. To feel certain, they need an agenda. Providing one puts you as the Sales Warrior in the position of strength by moving them toward life improvement. Creating an agenda has two steps, discussed as follows.

Deliver Your Presentation Agenda

A great way to think about this step is to imagine a launch pad between the 5 steps to understand your customer's mission, and the 4 steps to present solutions. The 5/4/3 Factor sets you up as the leader, and this step shows your prospect exactly what is coming next. Again, everything is about providing certainty that you have the best possible solution.

As you know, the most important thing in selling is having a position of strength. The agenda statement keeps that position of strength alive. Whenever a customer starts to work with the salesperson, there's always a question of whether the value is greater than the cost of change. The customer could also wonder whether the conversation adds value greater than what he or she could do online. This step is naturally evolving to ensure that the value we're giving the customer is greater than the cost of change.

Your goal is to let the customer know you are going to compare your solution to what the customer already has, other options under consideration, and the ideal option. You are showing the customer why what you offer is better than the rest and why you align with the customer's ideal.

State Your Goal According to Category

This is the tailored part of the agenda where you address the specific category. Remember, the Category 1 buyer is the true just-looking buyer, where they haven't decided to make a change. The Category 2 buyer is the overwhelmed buyer, where they have decided to make a change, but they haven't made many key decisions yet. And the Category 3 buyer is the torn buyer, where they have narrowed it to a few options and are deciding between them.

With a Category 1 buyer, the just-looking buyer, you could say something like this: "As I present some different options to you, my goal is that by the end of our conversation, you will be able to decide whether it is best for you to keep doing what you are doing or to make a change."

With a Category 2 buyer, the one overwhelmed, you'll say, "My goal is to narrow down your options, so that by the end of our conversation, you will know which _____ is the best path forward for you." (You'd fill in the blank with the type of company.)

And if the buyer belongs to Category 3, the torn buyer, you'll say, "My goal is to show you how we are different from the other options you are considering and to guide you to a place of resolution, so that by the end of our conversation, you will feel resolved with who you want to move forward with."

What's Up, Doc?

Think about the last time you went to a doctor. The entire process is designed to be outcome-oriented from the minute you walk in the door. You fill out the paperwork to let the doctor know about your current state. You tell the doctor how you are feeling, and the doctor walks you through the entire process. The doctor gives you certainty.

I share that with you because *you* are the sales doctor, and your prospects are those people locked in a state of uncertainty. They are trying to diagnose their own problems, and they can't do it. That's where you come in. You must be that sales doctor to give them the certainty that they need by mapping your agenda to the category of buyer they are.

The buyer *wants* you to be a Sales Warrior and wants you to lead. One of the beliefs of a Sales Warrior is that the rule of selling is to make it easy for customers to spend money and improve their lives. That's what you are doing by setting the agenda.

Any time we can provide a process or a path for people to follow, it lightens the mood and takes any mystery and suspense away from the conversation. We don't want mystery and suspense when our customers are spending a lot of money.

If you are working with a Category 3 buyer, then you might be hesitant to compare your product or service to the competitors. In the Discovery 360, you asked about what prospects have already seen. Now it's showtime—in this step, you will map out where you provide more value than everyone else. Your prospect *needs* you to do that. Remember, the biggest competitor you have is not actually your competitor; it's the conversation you are not present for. Your prospects are not the expert. They don't have the knowledge or confidence that you do. That's why you must help them work through the process to give them that certainty.

You already know that you have advantages, and you have weaknesses. But so does your competitor. If you are the one taking the prospect through the process of comparing in an aboveboard way, then you have the advantage, and you will make the sale. Hesitating with comparing yourself to the competitors is a huge leash that you will want to overcome, and the best way is by not focusing on yourself and instead focusing on your prospect.

One of the most common leashes B2B sales professionals have is reflected in the statement "I don't want to waste my time with stakeholders who aren't direct decision-makers." A mistake salespeople make in complex sales is to stop selling to someone after finding out that the person isn't making the purchasing decision. What effect do you think that has on the contact? It makes the person feel unimportant, and so now he or she is not a fan of you. You have created an adversary. Furthermore, the individual may not be a direct decision-maker but could have a secondary role in the decision. If your energy towards them said, "You are not important enough for me to talk to, so connect me to someone else," then you are a Warrior that just used your words and energy to shoot yourself in the foot. That's not the Sales Warrior way; Sales Warriors believe everyone is enough. The person in front of you is your prospect. You could recruit that person to be on your team to sell.

If you feel ready to take your agenda-setting to an advanced level, I want to share with you an NLP technique called the Infinity Loop. This is one of my most-used strategies to stay in rapport with a prospect, especially when starting a follow-up conversation. The Infinity Loop has four steps:

1. Remind your prospect what you both have discussed or accomplished so far.
2. Tell the prospect what you are going to accomplish together today.
3. Tell the prospect what you will accomplish in the future.
4. Circle back to your agenda for today.

You could move through the four like this:

(1) Thank you for joining the Zoom meeting; before we get started today, let me say that last time you said you wanted to stop blank and start

blank because of the blank outcome that you are wanting. When you achieve this, it will mean blank to you. (2) Today, I am going to present three options for you that are all great choices, and they all will accomplish your goal of blank. My intention is that you move forward with the option that feels easiest to start today. (3) Then, I will go over our operations and implementation plan for you so that we start achieving our brand promise of _____ for you, and then in six to twelve months, you will look back on this moment and say this was the best decision you ever made. (4) But it starts with going through these three great options and deciding which one is best for you to move forward with today.

Anybody who has watched me on sales presentations knows that I constantly set and reset the agenda. I always say what we have accomplished so far and where we're going next, and that's because it keeps me in rapport. And remember, when rapport is lost, all is lost. When you set an agenda and follow it, your prospect is going to subconsciously say, *I can trust this person. I can trust that the person is going to follow through. I can trust the person to take me down the path the way the person says.* Setting the agenda is a way to subconsciously build that trust. Tell prospects what you are going to do and then do it! And if you are lucky enough to have many prospects at a time, setting the agenda also keeps you on track. It is efficient because once you are seasoned, you can review your notes and set the agenda at the same time. So, you are preparing for your call while also setting the agenda and preparing the prospect for your conversation.

Another strategy when setting agendas between the different categories and decisions you are leading your prospect to solve is to use *next*. The word is the glue that holds all the decisions together, and you can really *next* your way throughout the entire process:

- "Now that you agree that blank is right for you, the *next* thing I want to do is talk about _____ or show you _____."
- "So now that you realize that this is the right decision for you, the *next* thing I want to do is talk about _____ and show you _____."

You can lead prospects all the way to the end. At the very end, you say, "The *next* thing I want to do is present three different options for you, and we'll talk about the advantages and disadvantages of each. And then, I will ask you to pick out your favorite. And then the *next* thing we are going to do is talk about what is holding you back from moving forward and going with us."

You could then say, "So now that you have decided this is the right overall option for you, the *next* thing to do is decide the timing. Would you like to get started today? Or get started tomorrow? Which would work better for you?"

The point is to remember you can always *next* prospects all the way to the end. Even with that last hand-off from sales to operations, you can say, "Thank you so much for choosing to be a partner with us. You are in great hands. The *next* thing I need to do is get operations people on a Zoom meeting with us, and they will go over the new client start-up process, so you are certain on how we are going to deliver on our shared goal of blank."

One of the most powerful techniques a person can do in selling is setting agendas throughout the sales process. Selling is all about momentum, and you have to constantly build it along the way because momentum is the foundation for building the value that's greater than the cost of change.

The 4 Steps to Present Solutions

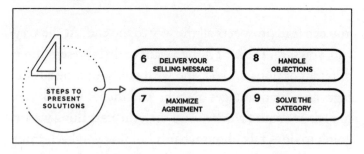

CHAPTER 10

Step 6: Deliver Your Selling Message

As a company, our vision is that we are engaged, responsive, and essential to our customers, and before Warrior Selling, we had never been professionally taught to show customers that. We were not truly "understanding the customer's mission." We now have a much more focused, disciplined approach.

—Jim, manufacturing

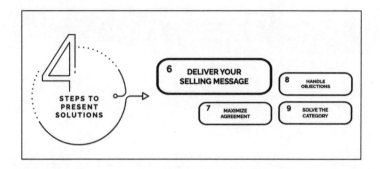

ENEFITS TO THE customer: Gives the customer complete knowledge and understanding of how your product or services will benefit him or her.

Benefits to you: Gives you an opportunity to sell your product or service and educate the customer on your unique value.

You already know that what you sell solves problems and improves lives. But is your selling message communicating that in a way that makes your prospects lean in? Is it making them tune out everything else going on in their brain to give you undivided attention? Or is your message just noise to them because you are saying the same thing that your competition is saying?

One of my favorite scenes in a movie ever is from *Walk the Line*, when Johnny Cash first walked into the audition room at Sun Records. At the time, he was a nobody. He sold appliances door-to-door and played gospel songs at night with two buddies. He was broke, and his marriage was in ruins. Scoring a record deal was his last and only hope. If you were standing in that audition room, you could certainly empathize with Cash's choice to sing a gospel song. It is what Cash knew best. What is more, gospel was popular in 1954. The audition doesn't go as Cash planned. As Cash begins to sing his safe, steady, dreary gospel song, the record label owner listens for about thirty seconds before interrupting: "If you were hit by a truck, and you were lying out there in that gutter dying, and you had time to sing one song—one song that people would remember before you are dirt, one song that would let God know how you felt about your time here on Earth, one song that would sum you up—you tellin' me that's the song you'd sing? Or, would you sing somethin' different, somethin' real, somethin' you felt?"

If you have seen the movie, you know what happens next. He flips the switch. He becomes Johnny Cash. He puts his whole soul and self into *his* own song. He completely loses himself rocking out to *his* song, "Folsom Prison Blues," and walks out of the audition room with a record contract.

The death of a sales professional is sameness. You can either disrupt the pattern of sameness by lowering your price or by saying something in a way that your prospect can't help but listen. The problem is you are about to ask your prospect to spend more with you than what he or she is currently spending and what the competition is charging. How can you do that if you are singing the same song the competition is?

You must create your selling message to stand out, to carve a niche inside your prospect's mind. You must create your selling message as if you have one shot to say what you need to say, as if you are never going to speak to this person ever again, as if the person will make the entire purchase decision based on your selling message. If the prospect was categorized as Category 1 or 2 and you set an agenda to determine whether the prospect should leave the current situation or whether what you sell is right for the prospect, then you will want to create a selling message around your product. However, if you have determined that your prospect is a Category 3 buyer and is moving forward with what you sell but trying to determine whom to purchase from, then you will want to create a selling message around your company. And the most effective way to structure these selling messages is with the VETO method.

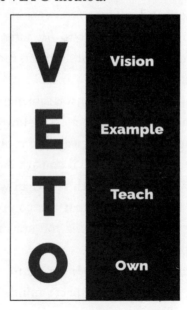

VETO stands for vision, example, teach, and own. The *vision* is the *why*—a provocatively respectful, tweetable line that engages a different space in the prospect's brain to produce new thought. The *example* is the *whom*—the proof of whom your product or service has helped. The *teach* is the *how*—the steps you use to execute your vision for your client, your unique process or method that makes your brand promise come alive. The *own* is the *what*, what your product or service will start doing for your customer. What will it do for the prospect personally and professionally if moving forward today? The *own* piece gets your prospect to mentally and emotionally take ownership before physically owning the product or service.

In this step, you are vetoing your prospect's current perspective. The prospect's current paradigm, based on experiences, shapes what is believed to be possible when solving the problem. This is your shot to completely blow the prospect's mind by showing an entirely new way to fix the problem. Maybe you are not on your prospect's radar as a solution. Maybe the prospect has heard about your company but doesn't understand how you are worth what you are charging. Or maybe the prospect is more sold, out of ignorance, on your competition or the current way of solving the problem. Either way, your purpose with delivering your selling message is to change the perspective. That happens by starting on an emotional level with your vision, giving an example of how that vision will benefit the prospect, teaching about how you'll solve the problems, and then letting the prospect take *ownership* over that vision by showing what life improvement will look like once you are chosen.

Every purchase is made with a combination of emotion and logic. The bigger the purchase, the more emotional it will be. Why is this important for your selling message? The brain is made up of two halves. The left side controls all your rational, analytical thought. This is the *what* part of the brain. The right side of your brain controls your emotions *and*—most important—your decisions. The emotional processor is constantly controlling the buying decisions your customers are making in their brain, *not* the logical one. Buying decisions are controlled by feelings like excitement and the vision of their future with your product or service. That's why every step of your presentation is focused on a vision first.

We created VETO in that letter order for a reason. It starts from the influence curve, which is how we create all of our lesson videos and training materials at FPG. We realized that the most influential commercials and brands you can think of all follow this influence curve. They have a philosophy, an example, a story, evidence, an approach of how to do something, and an application for what that something means to you. Everyone who has been in our training knows that this is exactly how we teach in the classroom and through videos. We give an initial philosophy, provide examples, share the steps on how to do something, and explain how that something works for our clients in the real world.

Why is it important for us to cover all four pieces? It's because a lot of trainers teach the salespeople to just show the *why* or the vision, to just give an example, or to just show the benefits. All that information is great, but we are all different and want to learn differently. Some want to hear about philosophy and the big picture. Some want to spend all day learning about the details. Some are more drawn to hearing examples and testimonials. The influence curve covers all the bases.

We need to cover each of the learning styles so we can reach every person in our classroom. You will want to sell this way because you don't know the convincing style of the customer you're talking to—and you may have multiple buyers with different styles. So I'm going to go through each piece of the VETO to build your selling presentation.

Vision (Why)

After you work through the five steps to understand your customer's mission, your first goal is to bring your selling message to life and to give your prospect an emotional connection to the choice you are selling. The vision is critical because it's the big picture behind your presentation, that one sentence that shows your prospect the *why* behind everything. The brain thinks in concepts first, which means you need to supply that so everything else will fit into it. If you just start rattling off facts and figures about your product or service but don't give your prospect a big concept or vision behind *why* you do it that way, all that information gets lost. The brain needs a place to put it.

The vision, the conceptual bucket, has two parts: your overall vision and why that vision benefits your customers. You are creating this vision for them around *why* you do things a certain way and the benefit to them for doing it that way. More than that, you are painting a picture for them of *why* your choice is the best possible solution. That will give them certainty and an emotional connection to your selling message that goes beyond a simple fact-based presentation.

Here are several ways that you can start your vision statement:

- "The people who choose (us, this product or service, to buy in this economy) have different priorities, they want _____."
- "My founder was sick and tired of blank in blank industry, so she decided to fix it by _____."
- "The vision of our company is to disrupt the blank industry by _____."
- "You're not going to believe what I am about to say, but _____."
- "When my architect created this floor plan, he did it with blank in mind."
- "When our company founder left Microsoft, he realized there was a huge need for _____."

Example (Who)

Once you declare your vision, you can immediately back it up with evidence supporting it. When influencing someone, remember what matters is what you can get the person to believe, not just what you believe. And the first step to getting people to believe what you believe is by proving your claims through evidence. Customer reviews, case studies, and statistics increase your chances of changing someone's beliefs. Collectively called *social proof*, they create immediate credibility in the eyes of the customer. Robert Cialdini coined the term in his 1984 book *Influence: The Psychology of Persuasion*. Customers want to feel safe and certain that they are making a good decision, and seeing the evidence of that through other customers helps them do just that.

Teach (How)

The *teach* element stands for *how* your product or service will accomplish the life improvement you've discussed. It is based on teaching something new and solving hidden and admitted problems.

In your presentation, you can add value and take the lead by teaching your customer something previously unknown. This is the absolute *best* way to position yourself as an advisor throughout your presentation. You are selling extra value when you show how your product or service will improve the prospect's life. The more you teach about things the customer didn't even know were needed, the more that person will want to spend more money on them. You are creating more value.

When I went to buy a car, I didn't know I needed a car with air-conditioned seats until I experienced the value of that during the presentation. Then this whole solution opened up to me that I didn't even know existed. Just the same, you are the expert on your product or service's value. Teach the customer something new, and you will be able to charge more for it. And that means having complete knowledge behind the value, so you can sell it.

Own (What)

Lastly, you show your prospect *what* your product or service will do for them in their world. You make your general selling message super applicable for the prospect. In the Discovery 360, you found out two vital pieces of information: what the customer doesn't like about the status quo and doesn't like about what the competition offers. That creates the basis for the problem and is what you zero in on as you work through your presentation. Show what is missed when the prospect doesn't have what you are selling.

The entire purpose of the final message is to get the prospect invested emotionally. How will the prospect use this product or service? What will it do to improve his or her life? Who else will be impacted by the purchase? Once the customer takes ownership of your product or service, how will it be used?

Here is how your VETO would flow together:

- Vision: "The vision of our company is to disrupt the blank industry by _____."
- Example: "For example, XYZ decided to choose us when it realized blank, which returned blank percent on their investment in the first twelve months."
- Teach: "The five ways we were able to accomplish that for XYZ and for you were blank, blank, blank, blank, and blank."
- Own: "Assuming you were to start with us today, here are the three ways it would work for you: blank, blank, and blank."

You will need to create a VETO message for every major decision that your prospect needs to make. You are going to veto the customer's current perspective around each of those decisions and veto the customer's expectation about what you are going to offer or even what the prospect thinks is needed to solve the problem. This is a pinnacle moment because if you are charging more than the competition, this is your opportunity to show that the people who spend more believe in your VETO.

CHAPTER 11

Step 7: Maximize Agreement

This simple step greatly impacts the rest of my sales process. When I maximize agreement, I know what I need to address further and what is going to keep the sale moving forward. It provides a level of confidence. So, it reinforces that you have to be able to talk not only about your product but [also about] the competition's product.

—Ed, industrial distribution

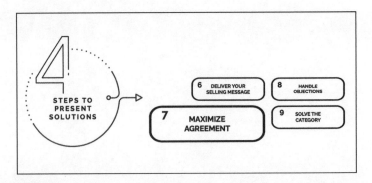

ENEFITS TO THE customer: Gives them a
360-degree picture of how what you are selling is
about to improve their life.

Benefits to you: Gives you the most position of
strength to create accountability for your prospect to
achieve their mission by choosing you over all alternatives.

As my father-in-law Blain Wrench says, "Selling is
about creating a basis of comparison." This step, the twin
of Discovery 360, does exactly that. The Comparison
360 asks questions based on current experience and
alternative solutions before you state your unique way
to solve the problem. At this point, you have given your
VETO, and now you need to compare what was *said*
to you in Discovery 360 to what you presented in your
VETO.

To assign value to something, we naturally default
to comparing it to something else because we don't possess an inherent ability to judge the value of something
in isolation. In NLP, this concept is known as mapping.

In this step, you compare what you are offering to
the prospect's current situation, what the prospect has

seen so far, and the customer's ideal vision. Does your product give everything liked about the current solution plus improve on everything that is currently not working? Does it have the positives of the competition without the negatives? How does what you are presenting compare to the ideal solution?

"I never thought of it that way" is the greatest thing people can say to me when I'm presenting my selling message. If you hear "It's better than what I envisioned; I didn't even know this existed," then that's the winner. I'm always striving for that statement.

The Comparison 360 is a powerful tool to get your prospects to see a 360-degree picture of how what you are selling is about to improve their life. This will give you the most position of strength heading into the eighth step, which is handling objections. Any possible objection that your prospect brings up will be able to be neutralized if you execute your VETO and your Comparison 360 correctly.

The Comparison 360 entails comparing the VETO you just presented in three key areas:

- How does this compare to the ideal solution you are looking for?
- How does this compare to what you currently have?
- How does this compare to what you have seen from other options you are currently exploring?

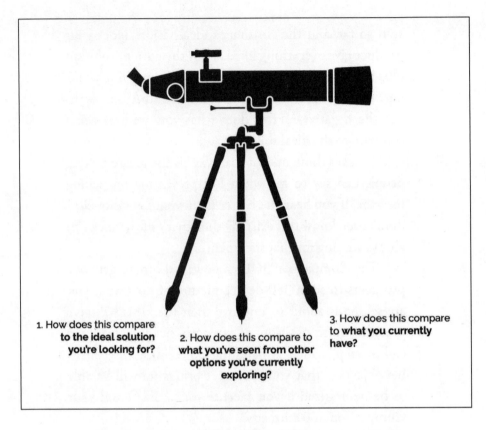

1. How does this compare **to the ideal solution you're looking for?**

2. How does this compare to **what you've seen from other options you're currently exploring?**

3. How does this compare to **what you currently have?**

You draw out two things here. First, you maximize agreement by getting the prospect to admit the ways you align with his or her ideal, how you are better than what the company currently has, and why you are the best option of all alternatives. Second, you gather vital data you need to handle any objections in the next step of the four steps to present solutions.

Let's face it—your prospect might not be completely sold on your product or service at this point and might still not fully understand why you are better than the competition or why you align with the ideal solution. And that's totally okay. The point of Comparison 360 is that you are getting the prospect to look more closely at the picture you just painted. Your prospect might really like some parts of it but might be unsure of others. Don't be afraid of that information; be grateful for it. Always remember that your biggest competitor is the conversation you are not present for. The Comparison 360 gives you a fuller picture of what the prospect likes about you, along with any questions or concerns. It allows you to control that conversation.

By this point, you and your prospect have learned so much about each other that you should feel comfortable asking these questions. If you have followed the steps correctly up to this point, you have built rapport and trust, and it would be unethical for you not to ask the questions. It would be unethical to let the prospect make the decision alone. Asking the comparison questions is the kindest thing you can do for your prospect, and it also gives you the intel you need to protect that person from the competition. You are protecting the customer from spending less and getting less, and you are a Sales Warrior who is advocating for your way of doing things.

You are always leading your prospects to the same conclusion. You always want their final answer to be "Yes, I choose you today." But they need to feel like they have the freedom to choose that path on their own with you positioned as their leader along the way. If your only question is "How is this better?" their brain will fight that. It puts their guard up because they feel like you are only allowing them to think and act a certain way. When you involve them in the process, their walls come down. They are more likely to give you a positive response because it feels organic. It allows them to put your unique benefits into their own words, without feeling like you are putting those words in their mouth.

One of the reasons this step is so powerful is because people don't argue with their own advice. You are getting them to admit out loud why you are in alignment with their mission better than anything else. But here's the key: What you say isn't ultimately what matters in the end. It's what you can get the customers to say. And if they vocalize that you are a better solution than anything else they have seen and better than what they have, *and* you are in alignment with what they are looking for, then there is no stronger position of strength than that.

As with Discovery 360, sometimes people are nervous about using the Comparison 360 to bring up the competition. Don't be afraid to hear what your customer likes about the competition.

Run toward that fear, and know that Sales Warriors are strengthened by conflict. By the end of the conversation, you are either going to move the sale forward or not. But you can't do anything until you know exactly where you stand.

CHAPTER 12

Step 8: Handling Objections

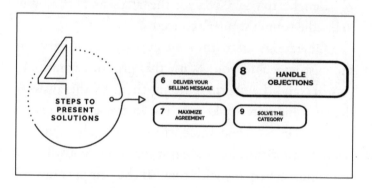

I was doing a demo for a customer on a machine that they had just purchased. Throughout the demo it became obvious that this machine had some maintenance issues. I had to think on the

fly. I used the three steps to handling objections with the customer, and then I immediately called a field technician to come out and get it fixed right away. At that moment the customer was able to see that even if there is an issue, I will get it fixed right away. It was a good example of if they have an issue after the purchase and out in the field, we can pretty much get there the same day and get them back up and running. We could handle objections the rest of the day smoothly after that.

—Craig, construction equipment sales

BENEFITS TO THE customer: Gives them an opportunity to bring up their concerns and have them handled.

Benefits to you: Gives you the fastest and easiest way to handle your customer's concerns.

Objections are within the customer, not between the customer and you. With this grounded outlook, you become the sherpa guiding them to the answers the customer already knows. For instance, if you get a price objection, what the customer is really saying is, "I really want this, but I am not sure how to justify the price; please help me with that." If the prospect says, "I really wish you included blank feature," what he or she is really saying is, "I really want to purchase your product, but I am concerned I will regret not having this blank feature." I find that it is always best to retranslate the objection this way, so you can handle what is really happening. In case you are wondering why I start each one with "I really want to purchase your product," it's because the prospect wouldn't be talking to you otherwise.

The only reason salespeople fear customer objections is because of one simple reason: salespeople make the objection about themselves. In other words, they take it personally. But a Sales Warrior sees it differently. The objections the customer gives you are just an internal conversation. So, when a customer tells you, "This just seems really out of our budget," that person is wondering, *Is the price worth the value?* When a customer says, "I'm just not sure; we're going to keep looking at our options," that person is thinking, *I just don't have enough certainty to move forward yet.*

This is a powerful and liberating belief for you as a Sales Warrior. Think about what this means—if it's not about you, then it's all downstream. Nothing is a fight, an attack, or a struggle. It's just a conversation you can guide to total resolution without a shred of fear. And one thing we know about the human brain is that it craves resolution. Your customers *need* resolution. They *need* freedom from their objections. And *you are* the Sales Warrior to give it to them.

I am all about being clear, assertive, and direct in identifying objections. It's extremely important to ask the customer, "What concerns do you have? What questions do you have? What would hold you back from saying that this is the right choice for you?"

I also want to address why I say, "handle objections" and not "overcome objections." I am very purposeful with these words. The word *overcome* suggests that there is a problem. The dictionary definition is "Succeed in dealing with a problem or difficulty." If I believe that the prospect is bringing up problems and difficulties, can I stay grounded, and is it possible for me to lead the prospect to find contentment in his or her internal struggle? Of course not. Labeling my prospect as someone bringing me problems and difficulties does not get me in the right energy to help. But the word *handle* is defined as "managing a situation." So, try on these two terms for yourself. Which one makes you feel more powerful, dealing with problems or managing a situation? My hope is that every time you hear "overcoming objections" or "handling objections," you remember that you get a choice in how to see the situation and what energy you bring to it.

Handling objections consists of following three simple steps; if you have followed the process up to this point, moving through them will be a breeze. The steps are discussed as follows.

Category 1: "What holds you back from saying that you are definitely going to make a change based on everything I've shared with you so far?"

Category 2: "What would hold you back from saying this is the right option for you?"

Category 3: "What would hold you back from moving forward with us?"

Acknowledge with Gratitude and Understand the Real Objection.

First, get on the same page by acknowledging what was shared with gratitude. For instance, let's say I get a price objection. I would first acknowledge that with a statement: "Thank you for sharing that you are concerned about that price." I repeat what I heard back and thank the prospect for sharing with me. This acknowledges that the prospect was heard. After I acknowledge with gratitude, I want to make sure I understand the real objection. My follow-up question can be specific: "Are you more concerned about the overall price or the monthly payment?" Or it can be general: "Tell me more about your concern."

The reason you want to dig a little deeper is that the true objection is almost never what the prospect initially says; it typically lies a little deeper. The trick here is to not get defensive or to give any response yet. Sharing with you a little longer can enable you to uncover any additional objections or the real source of the current discomfort. Think of this step as discovering the objection behind the objection. So, if the initial objection was the price and you asked the general question of, "Tell me more about your concern," the prospect might respond with, "Well, I'm just not sure about the economy right now, and with interest rates, this might not be the best time to buy." That's it—you just found out the real objection isn't the price, it's uncertainty about the economy. Now you can refine your message to fit the real objection.

It's so important that you acknowledge the objection because the customer has a high level of a stress hormone called cortisol. Objections can trigger anxiety, uncertainty, and worry. As a Sales Warrior, you need to step up by acknowledging the objection, which will give the prospect the confidence to ease that anxiety. If an objection is important to the prospect, then it's important to you.

Normally when salespeople hear objections, their amygdala hijacks them. They either fight, flee, freeze, or fawn. If you are a veteran salesperson, you might fight more because you know the right answer and how to explain it. When you don't acknowledge it and skip right to the explanation, you are going to come across as more aggressive and make the customer feel insecure.

Maybe you are new to sales and freeze up when you hear objections. Or maybe you take the flee approach by ignoring the objection altogether; the customer would then have a position of strength. Fawning, another approach, is when a salesperson verbally agrees with everything a prospect says in order to maintain the "friendship." Instead, you need to acknowledge the objection with gratitude. It gives you a moment to breathe before jumping to an answer, and it gives your customers certainty that you heard their concerns.

Failing to acknowledge and understand an objection will create a negative charge in your prospect. Think about how frustrating it would be to talk to someone who only cared about what he or she said and ignored everything you said. Those one-sided conversations are draining and infuriating, right? Then what happens? You either remove yourself from the conversation, or you zone out. People won't listen to you if there's a negative charge, and this step removes any such charge, so your prospect is open to listening to you. People will not hear your advice if there's an underlying negative charge. Don't be a conversation hog! Listen, acknowledge, understand, and *then* you can move forward.

Provide an Explanation and Get the Customer to Rethink Needs

This step gives your customer the *why* behind the way your companies, products, and services operate the way they do. If the prospect's concern is that you don't offer a specific service or feature, you can explain that it was a conscious decision to keep the cost down. If the prospect's concern is price, then you can explain the value and how your product or service checks off each item on the list of needs and that all of those items cost money. Your company decided not to cut any features in order to lower the cost because the people you work with see the value in each of those features. Now from the example, if you uncover the real objection is the economy, you can share why other prospects are choosing to purchase in this economy and the benefits they see.

After you provide an explanation, you need to maximize it by asking if the prospect feels differently now. The point is to get the customer to start doubting the objection. After you spend time presenting them with knowledge, you need to solidify that by asking, "So, do you agree that the current economy could be a favorable time to purchase?" All you need is a "maybe." That means the door is now open.

Get the Customer to Focus on Total Package and Resolve the Objection

The total package is everything you are offering versus what the customer is not currently getting. In the example, I can go back to the reasons why the economy is working in the customer's favor. That will help me overcome any remaining objections about my price. The goal is to reframe objections with regard to *everything* you are giving and to compare that to one or two features you aren't providing relative to other options under consideration. And then, you will solidify that by asking if the prospect feels good about moving forward past that objection.

One of the beliefs of a Sales Warrior is that a sale has compromise and collaboration. Remember, unicorns don't exist—no unicorn manufacturer, SAAS product, car, mattress, insurance policy, home, and so forth. As a Sales Warrior, your job is to get the prospect to prioritize his or her desires so you can help lead the prospect to the best-fitting option. Part of that process is guiding to compromise; without that step, the prospect will be set up for failure and not move forward with any option.

Sometimes, customers love to give objections all along the way, so you can use this step at any point in your sales process. The reason we have it here in the process is for those customers who aren't as comfortable sharing. They might nod in approval, but internally they have objections, so you need to ask. What you don't want is for them to not share with you, leave your meeting, and talk through their concerns with someone else. You would then lose all position of strength and have done the prospect a disservice. It is equivalent to a therapist's client smiling at the therapist while having a nice chat and then later talking to a friend about the depression. That friend, no matter how well-meaning, does not have the knowledge and expertise on how to fix it. It is imperative that you specifically and directly ask for objections because you are probably the only person who can guide the prospect to the best solution.

This step allows you to create the space and time to really understand the objections. Understand what snags might be present, regardless of whichever category you have assigned to the prospect, so that you can work through them together. You have worked through so much together already that this should be a very downstream conversation.

You may have been taught by sales philosophers that you don't want to bring up anything negative. As trainers, we teach that you *should* bring up something potentially negative and ask for objections directly: "Tell me what is holding you back. What concerns do you have? What questions do you have? What reservations do you have?"

You need to show your customer that you are confident in your ability to handle their objections. You, as the Sales Warrior, need to allow that space. Objections are almost always there, and by not bringing them up, you can bet that your customer is going to talk to somebody else about them.

Every serious buyer has objections; it's not a big deal. I love when I hear an objection because I know my prospect is seriously thinking through what it would be like to work with me. Think back to when you were truly just looking at a product; you more than likely didn't share any objections with the sales professional because you weren't emotionally trying it on to feel how it would fit in your life. In contrast, think back to the last big purchase you made. How many questions and concerns did you bring up? You probably had several as you were trying to decide whether you could purchase and whether you and the product were a match. Nothing's wrong with the prospect wondering if he or she should move forward. A wondering stage and a concerning stage always precede the buying stage; it's natural. Salespeople tend to put too much meaning on whether objections are good or bad. Objections are simply a sign that you are moving the sale forward, so releasing that charge and talking about them up front changes everything.

The stall technique is great for handling objections. A lot of times, early in the process, prospects are going to give you an objection that you are not yet ready to handle. Maybe you aren't sure what to say, or you just haven't been talking to them long enough to build up rapport. Or you don't have enough value to create enough total packages to handle that specific concern. When that happens, you can say, "Thanks for bringing that up. I've written that down, but let's continue talking through what we can offer you. And if everything else we discuss works for you, then I promise we'll come back to that concern."

Similarly, you can use a couple of approaches if your prospect asks for pricing early on:

- "Let's see if this is even the right fit for you. If you end up falling in love with what I show you, then we can go through all of the specifics of pricing, but if you quickly know this isn't for you, then I haven't wasted your time with the financing."
- "Oh, it's high. We are one of the most expensive in the industry, and we believe that you can charge more if you give more. We are all in and give the most compared to anyone. So, let's see if we are a good match; if so, I will put pricing together for you. But, I did want to be upfront and let you know that I am sure I will be the highest bid you collect.

Both of these stall on the answer. Early on, you often don't have enough value or haven't had enough time to know the prospect to be able to get him or her to rethink the needs or to focus on the total package. In those instances, stall, gain value, and then come back.

For the 1 percent of the time that someone demands pricing, just give it to them. Don't fight or refuse—just surrender. Typically, I suggest giving a range. I always suggest erring on the high side, and it's easier if the price ends up being less rather than more. But know if the prospect demands pricing at the beginning of the conversation, then this person probably is not a great customer for you.

The main objective of the stalling technique is to maximize your benefits and minimize an objection you might not be prepared to handle presently. The stalling technique works on any objection you hear, and it pushes that objection to the back burner so you can handle it later. *You* are the leader, so you want to be able to address each objection on your terms.

If you want to increase your buyers' urgency, you need to be obsessed with handling objections faster than your competition. A direct correlation exists between the objections you hear and the sales you make. The more objections you hear, the more invested your buyers are. You have the opportunity to handle all of these objections. The salesperson who can handle the most objections is the salesperson that wins.

As it relates to the process, sometimes you get an objection for which you don't have enough sugar to help the medicine go down. For example, let's say that in the Discovery 360 the customer brings up an objection or concern, but at that moment, you haven't yet gotten to the VETO. You might not specifically know the basis of comparison yet. When building a better case, you don't have enough value built up yet to handle the customer's concern. So, you want to stall in that situation until you have built up enough value: "I know earlier you were concerned about blank because of blank, but now that you have seen and heard how we do things, how do you feel about this concern?"

If a Sales Warrior doesn't give the customer the truth and resolve objections, then the customer must do so alone, with outsiders, or with the competition. And then you have lost the advantage.

A leash you might have is that by spending so much time on objections, you are just inviting the customer to think negatively about you, which will hurt the sale. This is where it's so important to get your mind right during objections. Sales success is 80 percent psychology and 20 percent mechanics. I truly believe that handling objections is simple, but the psychology gets in the way. If you get your mind right and think of objections as something happening for you and not to you, then they become your friend, not your enemy. Remember, objections are nothing more than feedback, and feedback is the path to mastery.

Objections we have in selling, especially in B2B sales, commonly come not from the customer we work with but from other absentee buyers involved in the sale. After you finish getting your contact to focus on the total package, you will check if it is resolved by saying, "If I shared that with your partner, would he be okay with that?" Resolve the objection through the person who is with you. This works with gatekeepers as well. Remember, Sales Warriors always sell to the person in front of them, who might not be the decision-maker, but the decision-maker's appointee. Let the appointee know that you realize that person knows the decision-maker better than anyone, and you would love for the appointee to share any concerns the decision-maker might have. You will use the three-step process, whether it is with the buyer in front of you or with an absentee buyer, through the intermediary.

Here is dialog for an absentee buyer: "So, it sounds like you know your partner will have a concern about _____. So, here's what I want you to do. I want to share with you what I would say to them, and I'll handle their concern as if he or she were here." You would go through your three steps of handling the objections process through the person you are talking with. You want to build up the appointee's importance by suggesting that you believe that person is important and influential enough to speak on behalf of the other buyer. When you do that as if the absentee buyer were in front of you, you will move the sale forward 100 percent of the time.

CHAPTER 13

Step 9: Solve the Category

I used to assume that I had convinced the prospect to make a change but then would get ghosted by them. Now I category close them, create resolution, and close more deals.

—Isaac, heavy machinery

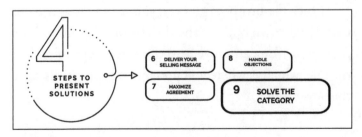

BENEFITS TO THE customer: Gives customer resolution on the previous category.

Benefits to you: Allows you to move forward down the most efficient path.

At this point, you will be closing out a category. And this is where a fork will appear in our perfectly paved sales path. Don't worry, you made it through the last fork by categorizing your buyer and setting the agenda based on the applicable category. And that is exactly what you will do again in this step.

The outcome of this step is to confirm that you have solved the category so you can transition your prospects to the next one. You will check in to make sure all decisions of a Category 1 prospect have been resolved so that you can transition the person to Category 2, which means going back to Step 5 and setting a new agenda.

So, if on Step 5 your prospect was a Category 1 buyer and your goal was to get the person to leave a current situation, you would have set the agenda by saying, "By the end of our conversation today, you will have a resolution on whether you should leave what you have." Now you circle back, asking, "After everything we have discussed, have you decided to definitely leave what you are currently doing?"

Once the prospect says yes, you set a new agenda of narrowing down options and do a second lap around the four steps. You can move into the three steps to resolve the sale, which is where you present your proposals once the buyer is in Category 3.

Now that you have the overview, let's get into more detail on how to solve the category. Solving the category means you are solving the decisions within that category that would prevent the prospect from moving forward with you. You want to move the prospect from just looking to overwhelmed to torn as efficiently as possible. It is only from being torn that the prospect can attain resolution.

At this point, you have delivered your selling message with your relevant decision VETO, you maximized agreement with the Comparison 360, and you handled any objections along the way. Before you move in for the close, you need to make sure customers are ready to see your proposal. Category 3 buyers are the *only buyers* who are capable of making the overall buying decision. If you show them a proposal before Category 1 and Category 2 decisions have been decided, then they will have too many objections piled on top of the price for you to be able to close the sale. At that point, the only resolution is for them not to talk to you again. Your objective is to maximize your probability of closing the sale. To do that, let's look at how to move through the different decisions in the next three sections.

Solve the Relevant Decisions

In this step, you're going to pull information from your Discovery 360, Relevant Decision VETO, and your Comparison 360. Whether your customer is in Category 1 or Category 2, you'll follow a simple formula with each

	CATEGORY 1	CATEGORY 2	CATEGORY 3
	THE 4 STEPS TO EFFICIENT & EFFECTIVE SELLING "CHEAT SHEET"		
STEP 1: DETERMINE	**The Just Looking Buyer** Has not decided to do something.	**The Overwhelmed Buyer** Has decided to do something, but doesn't know what.	**The Torn Buyer** Has decided to do something but is torn between 2-3 options.
STEP 2: OBJECTIVE	Lead them to "burn their boats."	Define their market and get them to narrow down to their 2-3 favorites.	Force the compromise to achieve resolution.
STEP 3: MESSAGE	"Why buy now..." "Why leave what you have..."	"Why buy this..."	"Why buy us..."
STEP 4: DECISIONS	1. Unsatisfied 2. Economic Climate 3. Financial 4. Emotional Urgency	1. Product	1. Competition 2. Circumstancial Urgency 3. Final Decision 4. Second Final Decision
		Brand	
	X- Factor		

decision: "You said you were struggling, worried, concerned, had questions about [use their words here to match the customer] with blank; we solved that in the following ways. Do you agree this solution will improve your blank?" You're echoing their problem back to them, showing them how your solution will solve that problem, and then gaining agreement on it.

Solve According to Category

You will want to solve the problem according to category:

- **Category 1 Close:** "When we first got started, you said you were not sure it was worth making a change right now because you felt your current blank was good enough. Then I showed you blank and how it would solve your problem of blank. How do you feel about changing now?"
- **Category 2 Close:** "When we first got started, you said you were overwhelmed and not sure how you were going to solve your problem of blank, but then I showed you blank and how it would solve your problem of blank. Do you feel certain that this [type of company] is the way to best meet your needs?"

With each of the categories closed, your prospect will say you either solved the problem or didn't. The prospect feels certain or not. If you solved the category, then congratulate the prospect and set the agenda for the next decision inside of Category 2 or Category 3. If you didn't solve the category, you will set the agenda for the next decision inside the category you are currently in.

Celebrate and Set the Appropriate Agenda

If your next decision is still in Category 1 (Unsatisfied, Economic, Financial, Emotional Urgency, X-Factor) or Category 2 (Product, Brand, X-Factor), then you will say, "I'm excited we were able to solve [list all that you solved already]; the next decision we need to discuss is blank." At this point, you are back at Step 6: Delivering Your Selling Message around that decision. You will continue to Step 7: Maximize Agreement, Step 8: Handling Objections, and then Step 9: Category Close. You will continue this loop until you advance the prospect to Category 3.

Your agenda statement for Category 3 is one of my favorites because it's proposal time. For that, you could say, "I'm excited we were able to remove that overwhelmed feeling by narrowing down your choices. Our next step is for me to present you with a proposal. Your proposal will have three great options based on your desire to stop doing blank, so you can achieve your goal of blank. How does tomorrow morning at 9:00 a.m., tomorrow afternoon at 1:00 p.m., or tomorrow at 3:00 p.m. look to you?" Of course, if you are able to go right into the proposal, then you would just say, "Have a seat in my office, and we can begin."

You may be thinking, *Jason, is it really necessary to close my prospects on all of these decisions before I get to the proposal? I could just give them my solution and send them my proposal—the end.* Here's the difference between a salesperson and a Sales Warrior. A salesperson is a transactional vendor who just sends the proposal and forces the prospect to work through all of the decisions alone. So, the salesperson may get a *market sale,* but guess what? Those prospects have an extremely high cancellation rate because they have unresolved objections or concerns. A Sales Warrior sees him- or herself as the primary source of confidence, motivation, hope, and certainty in the prospect's decision to buy or not. If you are a Sales Warrior, you will create *lifetime clients who will lead to a lifetime of referrals* when you resolve all their decisions. And the reason is because you are giving them complete confidence in your overall solution. You have no loose ends because you know that loose ends will eventually turn into buyer's remorse, bad client reviews, and cancellations. When you solve the decisions before you resolve the sale, you move from being another vendor to becoming their Sales Warrior advisor.

Sometimes I see salespeople who get overwhelmed trying to follow the exact order of decisions, but the beautiful thing about the 5/4/3 Factor is you can consciously move to any decision inside the category you are in. Whatever the most downstream decision is, that's what you should focus on next. Downstream means going to the most resistance-free, most natural next direction for the prospect. So, if the prospect wants to talk about the Financial Decision before the Unsatisfied, and the conversation naturally flows in that direction, go with it! Go with the decision that is easiest for the prospect to solve. Downstream means being flexible.

The Most Flexible Element in a Situation Controls the Situation

Being downstream is operating within the 5/4/3 Factor but following the path of least resistance with your customer while maintaining control. It's easier to move downstream than to swim upstream against the current. If you are fighting the current of the conversation, you are out of rapport.

What if you have a Category 1 prospect who already wants to talk about Category 3 decisions, like the price? First, you must acknowledge it and then either stall or be transparent and give the price. Then you reframe the discussion back to the relevant category. You would say, "Your investment would be $X. And the people who choose us have different priorities; they want to accomplish blank so they can [do, feel, achieve, become] blank. I am unsure if that's right for you yet because we just started talking, so let's get back to talking about blank, and then we can go back over the investment; once we agree, we can solve your problem of blank."

The customer doesn't know the fastest path to make the decision to improve his or her life. As the advisor, you need to acknowledge what was brought up, be grateful for what the customer believes is important, and then get back on track.

Finally, don't overcomplicate the process or skip steps or decisions. That will only lead to a lucky market sale, a future cancellation, or being ghosted. Just take it one customer, one step, one decision at a time. *If you choose to have the discipline to do this even when no one else will, then you will earn sales even when no one else can.*

The 3 Steps to Resolve the Sale

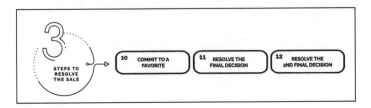

CHAPTER 14

Step 10: Commit to a Favorite

Using three options and labeling them has been a huge game changer in my sales. I get to maintain a position of strength and stay in rapport more easily during the closing process. I think it's fabulous. Those two words, resolve and certainty, really helped me in my mind to figure out how to get them to that point, so that was great.

—Elena, luxury retail

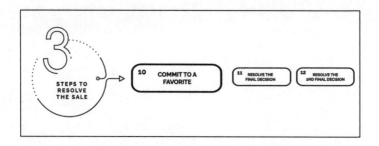

ENEFITS TO THE customer: Allows customer to remove an option and get clear on the advantages of the final two options.

Benefits to you: Positions you for the final close.

A direct correlation exists between your ability to ask a person to purchase and the amount of income that you earn. If that's the case, why wouldn't every salesperson ask every prospect to buy every single time? That's because of the salesperson's belief system and the related fear along the way. Another belief of a Sales Warrior is that performance (what the Sales Warrior does) equals knowledge (techniques and skills) minus leashes.

In an ideal world, that would be the entire formula. Once we've been told to do something, or we learn something new, that should immediately equate to doing it, right? But that's not really what happens, is it? Why don't we immediately execute the strategies based on the tools we've learned? Leashes hold us back. Internal rules, belief systems, or stories we tell ourselves keep us from using that knowledge all the time. So, realize that *closing is simple, but the psychology gets in the way.*

The closing technique I advocate might be different from ones you have learned because you will present not one, not two, but three options to your prospect. You should always present three options, with each being a good option that meets the needs of your prospect. People like options. In fact, most people need options in order to feel comfortable moving forward in a sale. Most times, a person's due diligence requires three options, so as a Sales Warrior, I want to do that work for the prospect and give three options that are all me. This way, whichever way the prospect goes, I win. Another reason I always want to give three options is that I know that with every sale comes compromise, so the options will have three different compromises. Typically, one option will offer every feature the prospect wants; the compromise will be the price. Then I will have one option at the exact price wanted, but, of course, some features and benefits have been removed. The third is an option in between. In my years in both B2C (business to consumer) and B2B sales, if I presented one option, I was going back to the drawing board and creating a new option and then another, and then the customer would move forward or be so exhausted by that point that I would get ghosted or have to wait weeks for another meeting to close the deal. In case you haven't figured this out about me yet, I don't like to wait. So, giving three options up front allowed me to close more deals that day.

Before we go over the psychology behind resolution, let's go through the simple steps to achieve it. The first step, commit to a favorite, has three phases.

Phase 1: Present the Benefits of the Three Options

Option 1 is always the highest price with the most features, option two is a step below that, and option three is the lowest price. When presenting your three options, you must deliver each with the same level of enthusiasm and admiration. Presenting the three options with no biases removes any resistance from the customer.

In the book *Influence: The Psychology of Persuasion*, author Robert Cialdini described the law of reciprocal concession. It means, in a nutshell, that if you present the lowest priced option first and it is outside the paradigm of what the customer can afford, and *then* you present the more expensive options, your probability of closing the customer on any of the options is dramatically less than if you start with the highest priced option and work your way down. The reason is simple. As soon as you present the highest-priced option that's way out of their paradigm for their price range, the lowest-priced option doesn't feel so expensive anymore. So going forward, commit to presenting your highest-priced option *first*, and watch your sales be unleashed.

I like to label each of the options. I make sure each label highlights what is best about the option, not what is undesirable. For example, I wouldn't label them as "priciest, middle ground, and cheapest." Instead, you could have fun with labeling them! Try the "life improvement package," the "scale-fast option," or the "growth package." Labeling has a huge influence on a brain.

Labels provide meaning and certainty for your prospect. In psychology, *decision fatigue* means that after making many decisions, a person's ability to make additional decisions worsens. The underlying cause of decision fatigue has to do with a person's stress levels and the number of decisions needed to be made each day. The weight of these decisions also matters. As a Sales Warrior, if you can make these decisions easy for your prospect by labeling them, that person is going to feel amazing moving forward with you. But if your prospect is already in a state of fatigue, you will be working against the person throughout the sale, which is why labeling is such a gift. You will take the prospect's emotional weight away.

Phase 2: Get the Prospect to Choose a Favorite

Here's where you deliver your Triple Bind, just like you did at the very start of the five steps to understand your customer's mission, by saying, "I'm curious. Of these three options, which one is your favorite right now?"

The prospect might say, "Well, based on these options, I really think option B would be the best choice for what we're looking for." The whole point is that you are narrowing choices down.

Phase 3: Get Buyers to Eliminate Their Least-Favorite Option

The last phase of this step is to keep narrowing options down even more. So, your next question will be "Which option would be least relevant for you so I can take it

169

off the table?" The customer might say, "Option C isn't going to work for us. There just isn't enough there."

If you are physically with them, then literally remove that option from the table, so that just two proposals remain. If you are on the phone or on a Zoom call, then just say that you are removing it.

Two options are still in play: option A and option B. Congratulations. You have once again moved the sale forward and are getting closer to complete resolution.

Another belief of a Sales Warrior is that the rule of selling is to make it easy for people to spend money to improve their lives. In this case, you are improving your customers' lives by making it as easy as humanly possible to decide.

A lot of salespeople I've worked with have struggled with this because they believe the customer should take the lead on the close. Whenever I go to conferences, I hear people teaching this mystical concept of buying signals. Buying signals are just rules you impose on the sales process to give yourself permission to ask for the close. And the more rules you have, the less freedom you have and the lower your conversion rate will be. For instance, I've seen a list that included a customer nodding his or her head and saying yes as a buying signal. That's crazy. There's no way to confirm that from prospect to prospect, and basing your entire close on something you don't know to be true will severely limit your sales. So, follow your process, stick to the steps, and don't be afraid of the word *no*. Remember, you are doing something *for* your customer, not *to* the customer.

Think about what your prospect is going through: searching the internet for solutions; having conversations with family, friends, or colleagues; and spending nights and weekends researching options. Your customers would give *anything* to have the certainty to get out of that. They want freedom, and you need to see yourself as the bringer of that freedom. Closing is easy; the psychology gets in the way.

What if you choose to not ask your customer to buy because you think, *I don't think the timing is right. I think I've taken up enough of the prospect's time. I'll find a time during our next conversation*? You have created harm in your customer's life because you have added more ambiguity. Now the customer must return to the current situation without any resolution and figure things out alone. The problem is that's not the customer's strength. By letting the prospect leave you without deciding, you are doing something *to*, not *for*, the prospect.

You ended the four steps to present solutions by solving the category, which means you have built three different options. Always remember: Having one option is no option, having two options is a choice, but having three options is freedom. With the three options, you give the prospect the freedom to pick the best, and you give yourself a better chance to move the sale forward.

CHAPTER 15

Step 11: Resolve the Final Decision

This step helped me realize that you need to ask your prospect if you're still competing with another company. It helped me realize that I had lost sales because I hadn't known they were talking to a competitor that was a cheaper price. Once I know they are talking to those competitors, I could show them that their machine is not as effective as ours, so our price is worth it. From there, I help them in trying to figure out if they can justify this purchase price; honestly, it's just conversations. So yeah, it

*helped me realize you have to identify this before
you can know how to close—such a necessary step.
—Justin, physical therapy and medical
equipment*

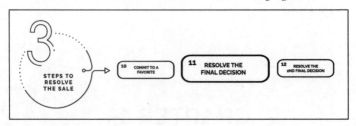

BENEFITS TO THE customer: Makes the customer feel wanted when asked to purchase.

Benefits to you: If all decisions have been resolved, you will be resolved, either because the customer closes or has decided to go in another direction.

Your entire selling process from your opening greeting has led to the point of asking for the sale. In the last step, you had your prospect eliminate an option, so two liked options should remain. Following the example, let's say your prospect has chosen option A (the most expensive option) and option B (the middle-priced option). Now you move toward achieving resolution with the assumptive close. Let's break down the phases of this step to ask your customer to buy from you.

Phase 1: Deliver the Assumptive Close
The assumptive close is so named because you want to assume that the customer has already chosen you and

is just trying to figure out which of the two options to choose from. So, you'll say, "Great, so it sounds like the choice is between option A and option B. Does that mean you have decided to go with us, and the choice is now just between those two options?"

You need to know if you have a competitor in play or if you are ready to move forward. The assumptive close is meant to remove any uncertainty with the customer at this moment and ensures you didn't miss something that you thought you had resolved.

If their answer is yes, then *congratulations*. You just successfully used the 5/4/3 Factor to resolve the sale. Next, you'll move on to Step 12 to get the customer to choose between your two options. When you get to this point, I always want you to take a moment for gratitude. I believe gratitude is the unyielding fuel for courage, and when you pause to be grateful for everything you have accomplished, you can do anything.

Most people experience some anxiety when making decisions, so your ability to deliver the assumptive close helps remove it. Decision-making happens in the pre-frontal cortex—the front part of the brain. According to research published in the *Journal of Neuroscience*, anxiety slows down and disengages the specific part of the brain needed to make decisions. As the Sales Warrior, you are *leading* people to decide. Your prospect is moving toward you by deciding or eliminating an option. No matter how skilled you are at handling multiple details, most people can only focus on one thing at a time. Narrowing things down takes advantage of the brain's natural tendency to see patterns and to organize and group information.

Phase 2: Sell through the No

If the prospect is still looking at alternatives, you want to stall so you can get a position of strength back. So, you will put talking about the competition to the side for now but know that you will return to it. Talking about the competition immediately gives all the position of strength back to the customer or the competitor. So, if the prospect says, "I'm still not convinced that we're going forward with you because I also really like XYZ company," then you will want to reply this way: "Thank you for sharing that with me. The good news is by the time we are complete today, you will feel 100 percent certain in what direction you are going and which is the best option. For now, let's go back to your two options with us and determine which is the best one for you."

When you hear that the prospect is still looking at other options, your body naturally reacts: your amygdala fires up, and you either fight, flee, freeze, or fawn. You end up fighting it by saying, "Who else are you considering?" And you lose your position of strength by giving the competitor the power. Or you end up fleeing by saying, "Oh, I understand—no problem! Let me know what you end up deciding." Or you freeze up and don't do anything. Or you fawn, saying, "Yeah, I can see why you would choose that company. It is really great, too, so either way will be great!" Each of those paths would immediately stop your sale. That's why you always need to sell *through* the no. You are constantly regaining a position of strength and working to maintain it. It's crucial not to take that bait, and you can fix it by making it all about your options. That's what gets you back to the position of strength. So instead of letting your amygdala hijack you, remember to keep your composure and keep the sale moving forward. Get the prospect focused again on what he or she likes about your options.

"So tell me, of option A and option B, which are you leaning toward?" Allow the customer the time and space to talk out the differences. Once it seems clear that the customer has a choice, confirm it. "You seem to like option A best, but currently it is too far outside of the budget. So today, the best option for you that meets your criteria and stays close to the budget is option B."

As soon as the customer states a preference for one of the two options, you can maximize your position of strength even more by eliciting the reasoning behind that choice in comparison to the alternative. That's your transition from Step 11 to Step 12, where you will then compare the favorite option with you to the option the competitor gave.

Let's go back to the Warrior Selling belief that the objective of selling is to make people feel wanted and to achieve resolution. By asking people to buy from you, you are making them feel wanted. You are communicating to them, "This was created with you in mind."

The biggest pushback to this step I hear is that buyers don't care about feeling wanted from a salesperson—they are making a purchase, not developing a long-term friendship, right? But their automatic brain doesn't make that distinction. Everyone has automatic emotional responses to certain behaviors, and the process I've outlined to deliver the close is one way to trigger that response of feeling wanted. So how might they feel wanted? You are more invested than any other salesperson in finding the right option that solves the most of the buyers' problems. You listened to their needs. Feeling wanted just means that you have given them the antidote to their indecision and ambiguity. And every single person you speak with wants that feeling.

That's how you make people feel wanted to achieve resolution. Your prospects are desperately searching for the option that solves most of their problems. By asking for the close, you are giving those two gifts. When people feel ambiguity, the amygdala's primal part of the brain fires up, leading to stress and anxiety, both of which stop sales. How do you avoid that? Actively understand their mission, give them certainty that you have the best possible option for them, and resolve the sale by proactively asking for the close. When you really believe this, you'll ask everyone to buy. Your sales will skyrocket, and your customers' lives will improve. You have that power, but first, you need the courage to push through and deliver the close with confidence and certainty.

Your job throughout this three-step resolution process is to keep the prospect focused on the fact that you have all the options. This will make you an advisor and not a vendor for your prospect, because you are constantly teaching something new all along the way.

Vendors are expendable. Vendors are salespeople who you don't trust or respect because they don't teach you anything new. They don't show you how to get from point A to point B. They haven't added any value. Choosing to be a Sales Warrior for your prospects involves leading, and that means following your resolution process and letting the score take care of itself. As a Warrior, you taught the buyer something new. You spoke with boldness and assertiveness, and you asked for the close. When you lead the prospect through the three steps to resolve the sale, the prospect will listen when you say, "Here is what I think you should do, and here's the reason why."

If this new way feels uncomfortable, realize that's only because you have done it a different way a thousand times in a row. Going forward, I want you to do two things when you feel that uncomfortable feeling as you are working through this new process:

- Have compassion for yourself if it's not easy right out of the gate.
- Practice until you can't get the process wrong, because when you lean into discomfort and create new myelin connections in the brain by

doing it over and over, you will absolutely watch your conversion rate be unleashed.

Resolving the final decision is critical because if you don't move forward in closing them at this moment and let the customer go, then you are giving the competitor an opportunity close. It's amazing how many sales I've made in my career from picking up where my competitors left off. You don't want to do all the work and have your competition get the sale.

CHAPTER 16:

Step 12: Resolve the Second Final Decision

I lost so much potential revenue by not doing this step. It just takes away your own biases, and you get to recap the journey. So, when you think about it, you want to make sure that as the Sales Warrior, you're addressing any pushback and creating forward momentum to understand their options. Then you show the objections worked through to explain and help them, so they understand that it's not critical anymore. Maybe something that was interesting or something that may be a concern is not that big of a deal when you compare it to all the other positives of the overall solution. . . . But ultimately, by using this step, you're able to get them to commit.

—*Brian, IT sales*

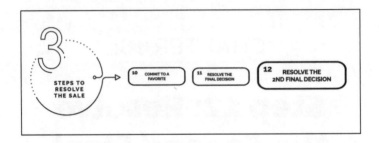

BENEFITS TO THE customer: Gives them final freedom by resolution.

Benefits to you: FREEDOM.

Everything in this twelve-step process has led up to this step. Once you have asked for the close, your prospect either said yes or not yet. Either way, this third and final step will give your prospect certainty to move forward with you. If they said yes, you will sell them on your two options. If they said no, then you are selling against your competition. Sales Warriors always run toward the competition, and this step will give you the science and the ability to do just that.

I created this second final decision because of a study I conducted. I asked myself, *How many salespeople push through a* no *during the close?* I observed one hundred different salespeople giving their selling messages. I found that 10 percent never asked their prospect to buy at all. And only 1 percent asked their customer to buy twice.

That means 99 percent of salespeople don't focus on the second final decision. You know by now that if you don't focus on something, you don't do it. You are learning how to become a top 1 percent Sales Warrior who asks a prospect to buy twice. You are learning why that first *no'* is really just a *maybe* in disguise. You are learning how to give yourself an immediate pay raise by closing your prospect twice.

Remember this: *The first* no *your customer gives you does not mean "no." Their first* no *means "not yet." You just have to change the way you see the word* no.

You must revere the word *no* because it means you are a step closer to handling a prospect's objections and making the sale. Let's say you only have thirty minutes to talk with a prospect and you wait until the twenty-ninth minute to ask him or her to purchase. You'd only have a minute left to handle that *no.* But what if you could get to that first *no* faster? What would that do for your sales? How many times could you turn *no* into *maybe* and then *yes?* All you need is more time. I challenge you the same way I challenge my own sales team. How fast can you get all of the information you need so that you can start your three steps? Maybe it will be on a first call. If not, if you must go to estimating and then make a proposals-review call, make sure you are being thorough but also getting to pricing quickly, so you have plenty of time to handle objections. You always want to make sure you are leaving your prospect in a state of certainty and feeling accomplished.

I always ask salespeople this question: In your mind, when does the closing process begin? Some sales trainers teach that you have to "earn the right to ask for the order," you have to "earn the right to close," or "the closing happens at the end." In Warrior Selling, I teach that the closing starts in the very beginning. Closing begins with that original Triple Bind opening, and you are closing your customer along the way. There is no single close at the very end; there is only a last close.

At this part of the process, the customer has said one of two things: either they are definitely moving forward with one of your options, or that it is between one of your options and an option by the competition. So, let's begin with our process if they are trying to decide between two of your options. When you narrowed down the options to two, you might have thought you were done, but that would be too easy. I believe that you never stop selling until the prospect calls it quits. Next, guide the prospect to the higher-price option that meets more needs. And then once the prospect says yes, upsell again. Never stop selling until the customer stops buying!

Be prepared with what else you can add on. If the customer chooses option B because of cost, see if you could add a part of option A to Option B. Be ready with ideas and the prices so you can resolve all of these decisions in the same meeting. I like to always make sure that I am congratulating the buyer along the way—after the decision between the two options and then with each additional add-on the buyer says yes to.

Here's an example of dialog for the final step through the resolution process:

1. Here you'll gain a position of strength: "Great! Now that you are definitely going forward with us, let's figure out which option is the best for you."

2. Next, you'll ask, "What is holding you back from choosing option A today?" Remember, option A is the more expensive of the two options, so you are focusing on removing any barriers to making that decision. Here, you'll get that first objection, which will mostly be about price.

3. Follow up with, "Let's say I was able to resolve that concern for you. What else is holding you back from moving forward with option A today?" Keep asking until the customer has no more objections. Make sure you write down each objection you hear. You'll use this list as your agenda as you go through each one.

4. Next, work through the three steps of handling objections with each objection.

Cross off each objection as you handle it. When your prospect is in front of you, doing so gives a great visual of how you are adding value, and it gives you gratitude for how you are moving the sale forward.

5. Summarize the process and close the buyer again. You could say, "You said these things were holding you back from choosing option A today. We've resolved each one, so the only thing left for us to do is to move forward and make this yours."

My favorite part about the upsell opportunity is an energy shift. When the customer says, "Yes, I definitely want to go with option B," I can feel a shift happening within me. The deal is done, and now I have all the position of strength in the world! Now, it's just a matter of presenting the benefits of the upsell. It's energizing! It's fun! You have already won. Now it's just about winning *more*.

Now for the next option. In this scenario, the prospect has chosen one of your options but is still considering an option from the competition. First, you need to ask what your competition has offered. Most of the time, your job is to help the prospect compare apples to apples. I always ask to see the competitor's proposal so I can put it side by side with mine. Now you can evaluate line by line. Almost every time during this process, you ask, "Are you okay with not having blank feature? XYZ company is not including it." You will use the three steps of handling objections to answer each concern. One thing to remember here is to keep your energy neutral. Right now, you are their advisor, helping the prospect to make the best decision. From that energy, you can easily and freely ask if the person is willing to give up so many wanted things just because of cost.

Perhaps you don't offer something that the competitor does. Explain the reasons why. You need to know the history behind what you sell, what you don't sell, and why. If you don't know what it is, find out. Armed with this knowledge, you can discuss with your customer what the person wants from the competitor and likes about those aspects and how you can fulfill that need in a different way.

At this stage, it's important for you to stay outcome-focused. Keep reminding your customer of the outcome, of the *why*. Forget about the problem for now. Why did the customer want your product or service? What is the desired outcome?

This is an example of how the second final decision will sound if the customer is choosing between you and a competitor:

1. "Tell me what you love about us that you don't get with the other options you are currently considering." You want to express this because you want to get a position of strength back by having the customer highlight your advantages over the competition.

2. "What is holding you back from choosing us today over Competitor X?"

3. "Let's say I was able to resolve that for you. What else is holding you back from buying with us today?"

4. Remember, these are the three steps of handling objections, so just work through however many objections they give you one by one, crossing off each one as you go.

5. "Great! You said these things were holding you back from buying today. We've resolved each one, so the only thing left for us to do is to move forward and make it yours."

You must get the science down first, so you can add your own art to the process later. I promise you that when you focus on resolving the second final decision for your prospect, you will become the top 1 percent Sales Warrior.

The leashes that salespeople have are usually just the result of not having a process to follow. Your brain is a processor, which means it learns and grows by following a process. Your brain is great at convincing you that something isn't possible when it doesn't have a process. That's exactly what happened to a client of mine named Victor. When I first talked to Victor, he was part of the 10 percent who asked for the close once, but he was also part of the 99 percent who didn't ask for the close twice. I asked him why, and he said, "Jason, I don't know what else to say without sounding needy or pushy." I asked him, "What if I could show you a process to close every single prospect a second time?"

I taught him the three steps to resolve the sale, and that leash evaporated. Now he had all this certainty and confidence in himself, and he became a top 1 percent Sales Warrior just like that. All he needed was a process to close more customers, and these three steps gave him the certainty to do that. That same path to the top 1 percent is open to you as well. All you have to do is choose to become the Sales Warrior.

I want to give you one more final closing strategy. This one is so good it is going to have you loving me and cursing my name when you see how much money you lose by being in the highest tax bracket. Are you ready? Use this when there is a price objection, what you offer is higher than that of the competition, and the one holdup to signing your contract is the price:

> **Sales Warrior**: "I am curious—if both contracts were free, whom would you choose?"
> **Prospect**: "Jason, I would definitely move forward with you."
> **Sales Warrior**: "Great! What would make you choose me?"
> **Prospect**: "You have high accountability, you specialize in this field, I really agree with your philosophy on sales and Sales Warriors."
> **Sales Warrior**: "I love that; are there any other reasons you would move forward with me?"

189

Prospect: "Yes, I really like that you use assessments. I haven't found another recruiter that does that. And I really like that you proactively go after top sales-people to recruit instead of waiting for applications to come in from jobless salespeople."

Sales Warrior: "Yes, I am very proud that we do that too. Is there any other reason you would choose us?"

Prospect: "Well, I don't know, I mean, I feel like I can trust you, and I really like the idea of my new sales recruits being trained by you starting day one. Yeah, that's probably it."

Sales Warrior: "Thank you for saying all of that; all of the things you said are very important to us, along with how we can keep our brand promise of guaranteeing that our sales recruits perform better than 50 percent of your existing team. I only want to put systems and processes in place where I know I can guarantee my clients hit their goals. Without everything you mentioned, it is a crap shoot on whether the recruit is going to perform for you. But, as you can imagine, every reason why you want to move forward with us costs money. But I believe you can charge more if you give more. Do you believe that too?"

Prospect: "Yes, I know in my business we charge more than the competitors because we do more also."

Sales Warrior: "Yes, so does that mean that you feel comfortable moving forward at this price?"

Prospect: "I'll sign the contract now!"

This technique allows buyers to sell themselves on why you are the better option. People don't argue with their own advice, so if you can give them the space to articulate all the reasons they would prefer you, saying yes is easy.

What about the times when you do *not* close the buyer? I believe that by following this process exactly how it's written, you will have the highest probability of closing a buyer over those who follow any other sales process. However, this does not mean that you are going to close every prospect every time! Even the best baseball players don't hit every pitch, and that's okay.

If you take a person through this entire process, and that person still isn't ready to buy, you have still won. The goal is resolution, not closing. You can see this process is setting you up to close, so don't get me wrong. But I purposefully did not call this the three steps to close a sale. Resolution is the goal and gift for both of you. Not only do you give the prospect resolution, but you also give yourself freedom. No Sales Warrior loves endlessly following up with someone. If the person closes, that's great, and operations takes over. If the prospect decides to move forward with someone else, that's great, and you can move that customer out of your CRM tasks.

People naturally like to choose the easiest option that improves their life the fastest. All the work you have put in with the Warrior Selling process has made you the easiest option. If you have done the work, your customer trusts you. Everything that you have done has put you in an unrivaled position of strength, and if they still see the other options or spend time thinking, you are going to be the one to beat.

The step discussed in this chapter is about choosing to be in the top 1 percent. But to do that, you have got to have a strong, compelling vision. Take some time right now to answer these questions:

- What will becoming a top 1 percent Sales Warrior do for you?
- How will becoming a top 1 percent Sales Warrior benefit your life, your family's life, and your customers' lives?
- What is stopping you from choosing right now to become a top 1 percent Sales Warrior?

Life is nothing more than a series of decisions. You need to make the decision right now to become a top 1 percent Sales Warrior.

CHAPTER 17

Your Sales Warrior Send-Off

CCORDING TO THE United States Department of Labor, sales is the single largest profession in the United States. Yet a grassroots study revealed that just 18 percent of consumers have a positive view of the sales profession. Meanwhile, more than 50 percent of college grads are likely to work in sales at some point in their careers.[6] The final kicker is that less than 3 percent of the four thousand colleges in the United States have a sales program or even teach a single sales-specific course.[7]

This is a perfect storm. Sales currently has the most jobs, gets the most complaints, and provides its employees the least education of any major profession. It's no wonder people have been programmed to have such a dim view of salespeople. They have probably encountered a lot of bad ones.

This, unfortunately, has bled into salespeople's picture of themselves. They deny themselves respect because others have denied giving it to them.

I believe sales is the least respected job in the world, next to prostitution (really). People will go to crazy lengths to call themselves anything but a salesperson: sales consultant, product specialist, counselor, product officer, service representative, even results achievement specialist.

Sales Warriors are on a mission to bring the pride, purpose, and respect back to professional selling. Because this belief is their personal truth, their actions reflect it. They are advisors, not vendors, for their prospect's deepest needs. They want to solve their prospects' problems because they realize they are freeing them from ambiguity. This is the very definition of *noble*.

The Japanese samurai would meditate about their own deaths every morning and every night. They envisioned themselves dying in hundreds of different ways, every single day, without fail. Even if the practice seems morbid to us today, the outcome was psychologically important. By doing so, they could no longer be afraid of their own death. They became fearless in battle and were able to live in the moment with perfect bravery. In other words, if they took away their fear of death, nobody else could lord that over them, which allowed them to live fearlessly. The practice was never *really* about death at all. It was about personal empowerment.

Modern research backs this up. Reflecting on death can actually be a powerful vehicle for self-improvement in the present. A study by psychologist Adam Grant found that when people are reminded of their mortality, they become more productive and purposeful. In essence, they have removed the reactive tendency to be fearful.[8]

There's a concept I use all the time called the "no monster." Every salesperson has this intimidating vision of the word *no* in their head, to the point that it becomes an unconquerable monster. But really, *no* is just a word. And if you decide to be like the samurai and meditate on all of the ways people can tell you no, the harsh ways they could tell you they don't want to work with you and they will never buy from you, it will duplicate the "scariness" and allow you to sell like you are already dead. Every time you go into a selling situation, you have to believe that you'll never have another conversation with that prospect.

What would happen if you viewed every *no* as a *not yet*? Prospects just don't have enough value built up around what you sell. They don't yet fully understand why or how you are about to change their life. There's never a reason to fear *no* if you hear the objection as "I need you to keep selling me so I can truly understand how you are about to remove the pain I have right now and guide me toward life improvement." What would *that* do for your sales results?

Brandon Steiner, the founder of Steiner Sports, one of the most influential sports memorabilia companies in the world, staked his reputation on being bold. Before one pitch meeting, he found out the decision-maker's favorite sport was running, bought him a pair of new running shoes, and only sent him the left shoe with a letter attached: "Tomorrow when I come in and meet with you, we're going to get off on the right foot." He showed up the next day with the right shoe, and he closed the deal that day. That's how you sell, as if you are already dead.

At its core, this idea of becoming already dead is fundamentally about freedom, about freeing yourself from the tyranny of your fear, which chains you from your own progress. If you are disproportionately afraid of death, you'll recoil from any activity that conjures up that fear. At that level, even the morning commute produces fear-based anxiety. And that limits your happiness. Just the same, salespeople often have dozens of fears running through their minds at any given moment. "What if I ask for the sale and they say no?" "What if they don't like my sales message?" "What if they don't care what I have to say?"

The purpose of becoming already dead to your fears is to quiet all those what-ifs. The samurai lived as though they were already dead, which eliminated the fear of death. You can borrow this idea of becoming already dead to eliminate whatever fears are leashing you from selling like you were born to sell.

The way you do this is to simply sell as if you have nothing to lose. Because guess what? You don't. I make it a goal to walk into every selling situation with the mindset that I have nothing to fear. I tell myself, "I am strengthened by the word *no*." When I give into my fears, I'm also limiting my ability to help others. How often has that happened to you?

Having that mindset has to be a total shift from your current reality, but it's entirely possible. Every time you go into a selling situation, you have to believe that you'll never have another conversation with that prospect. You have to believe that there will never be another opportunity for you to make your pitch, to say that one more thing you needed to say to convince the prospect. How would that change your message? How would that add urgency to your push to improve the prospect's life?

This concept is relevant in just about every facet of modern life. In sports, you hear coaches and players tell each other to "leave it all on the field." In life, we often say, "Live life like there's no tomorrow."

Your goal at the end of every day is to be able to look in the mirror and convincingly tell yourself, *I did everything I could've done today to move the sale forward.* If you can't, you weren't selling as if you were already dead. You were overthinking and fearful of what *might* happen if you put yourself out there and everything goes wrong. That's a mental hijack.

Fear is nothing more than a state of excitement, and all excitement produces the same reactions in your body. Your heart rate increases, you breathe a little quicker, and your palms begin to sweat. Your reaction to being chased in the woods by a bear produces the same physiological response as if you were surprised with a check for $1 million. The only difference between fear and excitement is your attitude about it.

When you reframe your perspective about fear, it becomes a positive state of excitement. And that's how you sell as though you are already dead.

How would you feel if your prospect bought from your biggest competitor who is going to hurt or take advantage of the prospect or prevent the customer from accomplishing his or her goals? That's the Protector energy; add to that the lingering thought, *If only if I had said blank.* You got fired on the customer's terms. How does that make you feel?

If you are going to lose the sale, die trying. Lose with integrity, dignity, and honor that you said and did everything you could. As Mary Marshall Forrest says, "Speak your highest truth." Once you feel in your heart you have spoken your truth, then it's up to the customer, not you. You can sleep at night knowing you did everything. You can die completely. You conquered your sales presentation.

During the last football game of my senior year in high school, my coach looked around and said, "Only six of you will play college football. For the rest of you, this is the end. In a few hours, you will never play football again. My advice to you, play until the whistle blows and get all the football out of your system. Do not be a forty-five-year-old man who lives through their sons or spend their weekends watching football to relive their glory days."

That night, I gave everything I could, and when the game ended, I got on my knees and started crying. I knew my football days were done, but I had no regrets because I did what I needed to do. Football had died for me, and I had complete resolution and freedom that part of me was over. And I was open and free to begin a new chapter and start something new. I focused on my academics, graduated from college early with honors, and went on to own a successful sales recruiting and training company, speak to thousands of leaders and Sales Warriors, and write books like this.

Still, I have to wonder if my coach hadn't said what he said and I didn't play like I did, if I would have been pressuring my son, obsessed with my glory days. When I say sell as if you are already dead, it gets all the selling out of your system. Then you will feel that inner peace or freedom that I strive to feel at the end of every sales process regardless of whether the customer buys. I don't want you to carry the what-ifs of past prospects. If you do, then those past regrets will eventually make you weak, which will come across in what you do and what you say. Get the sales out of your system. This is how you can have a 100 percent conversion rate.

One more thing—I want to talk to you about what it means to have a warrior life. It's easy to be a Sales Warrior when you're at work, when you're with your prospects, and when you're working on your mission to improve the lives of your customers. But you need to remember that you're a warrior all the time. You don't turn some warrior switch off and on.

When you're a parent, you are not sometimes a parent; you are a parent 24–7. You're fighting for your children every single day to grow them into the best versions of themselves. If you were a doctor, you are not sometimes a doctor. If you see someone on the street collapse, you use your skills to help the individual, even if you're off the clock. When you're a warrior, you're a warrior in every moment of your life.

Certain people don't have a choice to have warrior moments, they have to—like first responders. Do you choose to have warrior moments or a warrior life? When you think about the military, doctors, nurses, the people on the front line putting themselves in harm's way, do you want them to be living for warrior moments or living a warrior life? Reflect on all the warrior moments you have had this year, like being an advocate for your brand, being strengthened by conflict, and advocating for your customer. These build your armor because a warrior doesn't rest until the war is won. What war is that?

Convincing every prospect that the biggest mistake of his or her life is not moving forward with you and your company because you believe so much in your value. You are in complete disbelief when someone chooses your competition over you.

Every time you remember that a *no* is really just a *not yet*, decide to run toward what other people avoid, and realize that some problem exists with the prospect's current product or service or else the prospect wouldn't be talking to you, embrace these moments. They start to run together, and you build a warrior life, lived by rituals, disciplines, and constant focus on the objective at hand. To be the ultimate Sales Warrior, know that it's not about having a series of moments; it's stringing them together until they are embodied. *Choose to not just have values but to become them.*

A warrior is all in, so be all in, wherever you are. When eating dinner with your family, listening to a friend, or watching your kid's soccer game, be all in. Give the same level of presence, attention, and forethought to all areas of your life. Give your friends and family three options. Summarize conversations back to them. Handle conflicts between people you love. Be their Leader, Protector, and Servant. Everyone has a warrior within them, and it's just a matter of choice. Choose a life of service. Choose a life of protecting. Choose a life of leading. Reflect on all the warrior moments you have had this year and use those examples every single day to become the ultimate Sales Warrior. Before I leave you to reflect on your warrior moments this year, I commend you for choosing this Warrior life because, as you know, it's not always the easiest path to take.

Thank you for the risks you take. Thank you for the jobs you provide. Thank you for the products and services you present to improve others' lives. Thank you for the solutions you advocate for that increase business, speed, and profitability. Thank you for the late nights. Thank you for the early mornings. Thank you for the missed dinners, kid's games, recitals, and plays. Thank you for the months when you don't sell anything at all, but you kept going. Thank you for the rejection you put up with for the sake of the company you serve. Thank you for giving certainty to your prospects, customers, and company during uncertain times. Thank you for constantly mastering your mindset, process, and language.

Without you, our customers wouldn't be buying during these times, and our country would be way worse off financially. *You are honored.* Keep being relentless. The world needs a Sales Warrior like you. This is Jason Forrest, and I urge you to push yourself to become a better version of you.

About the Author

JASON FORREST IS the CEO and the creator behind the training content and sales recruiting methodology of FPG. Global Gurus ranks his Warrior Selling and Leadership Sales Coaching programs second among the world's top sales development programs. His provocative style of speaking his truth ranks him as number 5 on the Global Sales Guru list. Jason is a master practitioner in neurolinguistic programming, the science of influence and behavioral change. He is also a practitioner in accelerated evolution, the psychology of removing fear in high performers.

Jason is on a mission to ignite the pride, purpose, and respect to professional selling by teaching the mindset, process, and language of a Sales Warrior.

Endnotes

1. Jason Jordan and Robert Kelly, "Companies with a Formal Sales Process Generate More Revenue," *Harvard Business Review*, January 21, 2015. https://hbr.org/2015/01/companies -with-a-formal-sales-process-generate-more-revenue

2. "World's Best Sales Development Programs 2022," Global Gurus, March 25, 2022. https://globalgurus.org /best-sales-development-program/

3. Jordan and Kelly, "Companies with a Formal Sales Process." https://hbr.org/2015/01/companies-with-a-formal-sales -process-generate-more-revenue

4. Karrie Lucero, "Sales Turnover Statistics You Need to Know," Xactly, June 17, 2022. https://www.xactlycorp.com /blog/sales-turnover-statistics.

5. Maluso, N. (2020, August 28). *It's turnover time for sales*. Forrester. Retrieved July 15, 2022, from https://www .forrester.com/blogs/itsturnovertimeforsales/

6. "Students—Think About a Rewarding Career in Professional Sales!" Sales Education Foundation. (2022, June 29).

Retrieved July 10, 2022, from https://salesfoundation.org/who-we-serve/students/index.php

7. "Teaching Sales," *Harvard Business Review* (2014, August 1). Retrieved June 28, 2022, from https://hbr.org/2012/07/teaching-sales

8. S. Dominus, "Is Giving the Secret to Getting Ahead?" *The New York Times*, March 27, 2013. Retrieved June 10, 2022, from https://www.nytimes.com/2013/03/31/magazine/is-giving-the-secret-to-getting-ahead.html

Index